Organic Wesley

Garrett,

Thankyou for all the many ways
you have shared your love +
support towards our garden,
church, + community. And
espaciely for our friendship!
I am so looking forward to
our continued plantings in 2016
and I believe this book
will feed + affirm our passion
in creation stewardship.
   It will be good!

Blessings,
Donna
12/2015

Organic Wesley

A Christian Perspective on Food, Farming, and Faith

William C. Guerrant Jr.

 seedbed

Scripture quotations are taken from the Holy Bible, New International Version®, NIV®. Copyright © 1973, 1978, 1984, 2011 by Biblica, Inc.™ Used by permission of Zondervan. All rights reserved worldwide. www.zondervan.com
Printed in the United States of America

Paperback ISBN: 978-1-62824-217-1
Mobi ISBN: 978-1-62824-218-8
ePub ISBN: 978-1-62824-219-5
uPDF ISBN: 978-1-62824-220-1

Library of Congress Control Number: 2015949076

Cover design by Nikabrik Design
Page design by PerfecType, Nashville, TN

SEEDBED PUBLISHING
Franklin, Tennessee
Seedbed.com
SOW FOR A GREAT AWAKENING

Contents

Neither is there any need that conversation should be unedifying, even when it turns upon eating and drinking. Nay, from such a conversation, if duly improved numberless good effects may flow. For how few understand "Whether ye eat or drink or whatever ye do, do all to the glory of God?"—And how glad you ought to be of a fair occasion to observe that though the kingdom of God does not consist in meat and drinks, yet without exact temperance in these we cannot have either righteousness or peace or joy in the Holy Ghost.

It may therefore have a very happy effect if whenever people introduce the subject you directly close, and push it home, that they may understand a little more of this important truth.

—JOHN WESLEY
"A LETTER TO A FRIEND" (1748)

Foreword

JOHN WESLEY WAS a giant of a man. He continues to cast his long shadow of influence across the world. Ten preachers of today could not fill his shoes. I remember the first time I met him, in the form of his life-sized statue. He stood staring upward with a Bible in his raised hand. I stepped up to him to say hello, and noticed that I was quite a bit taller. He was five-foot-three. Weighing less than one hundred and thirty pounds, he was as lean as a jockey. Wesley might not be surprised at our greater height today, but what about our girth?

I recently learned about a casket that is almost as wide as Wesley was tall. It's called "the Goliath", and it's a whopping four and a half feet wide. A few decades ago when the company started making this supersized casket, they sold one a year. Today they ship one out every four or five days. Cemeteries accommodate the Goliath by selling double-wide grave sites.

How did our waists get to be the size of giants? What happened to our diets, habits, and food to make the change that resulted in this growth? How does the change affect our souls? What would Wesley say? What would he do?

You hold the answer in your hands. Farmer, theologian, and Wesleyan author Bill Guerrant has been searching out the answers to these questions. His answers in *Organic Wesley* are a satisfying feast.

Bill examines the current state of our diet and agriculture, as well as Wesley's thoughts on consumption, food sources, and the treatment of animals in agriculture. We in the church will be richer for following along as his investigation unfolds. He starts with a survey of the current situation of our waistlines and where our food comes from. We learn that there are twice as many prisoners in America as there are farmers. He presents us with an engaging portrait of Wesley, the thought leader, who is as lively and challenging today as he was to his contemporaries.

I am particularly glad that Bill has thought through what Wesley would *not* be happy about in the current local and organic food movement. Bill warns about the narcissism that can come from worrying only about ourselves. In so doing, he heeds Christ's warning that we take no thought of what we eat and drink, realizing that life is more than meat and raiment. In the truest sense of Wesley, he keeps ever in mind that we should first seek the kingdom of God, and then all the others things of life fall into place.

Many in the church today would be hard-pressed to articulate a biblical ethic on food. But think about the number of times food shows up in the scriptures. When Eve saw that the fruit was "good for food" and couldn't control her appetite, humanity fell from paradise. Esau lost his inheritance because he thought with his stomach instead of his head. The Hebrew people on the Sinai Peninsula were willing to trade their newly won emancipation for the fleshpots of Egypt. Eli couldn't control his appetite or his son's, and fell off a wall like Humpty Dumpty and couldn't be put back together again.

Jesus fed thousands on the mountain and taught during supper for five chapters in the book of John.

He could turn water into wine, but he resisted Satan's tempting all-you-can-eat buffet in the wilderness and set a standard for temperance.

Ten years ago, when I first dug into what Wesley had to say about health and eating, I found it a challenge. I had not paid attention to my diet, and my waist showed it. Since then, I have adopted several habits to take better care of my soul and my body. I have eaten hundreds, even thousands, of meals with others. When I'm at a restaurant with a friend, I suggest that we split a meal, even if they order something I don't particularly like. It is far more important to share a meal than to feed my wants. I learned to see that I was not practicing the temperance which is a hallmark of a Christian, and cut back on soft drinks and snacking. The result is more fellowship and less thinking about myself—and I weigh forty pounds less!

The Bible says that in heaven the Tree of Life will yield fruit in every month and that all the nations will be healed. Paul cries out in an eternal joy and optimism, "Yet in this body will I see him!" It is difficult to picture standing in front of our Lord in a body that required a Goliath-sized coffin. Gluttony, lust, greed, and sloth are deadly sins. Tending the temple of our bodies with the food we eat is part of the serious business of being a Christian.

I am thrilled that Bill Guerrant wrote *Organic Wesley*. It is essential reading not only for those who admire John Wesley, but also for everyone who hungers for soul food.

Matthew Sleeth, MD
Author and executive director, Blessed Earth

Preface and Acknowledgments

AS I WAS nearing the end of my seminary studies, the time came for me to choose a topic for my thesis. After considering and abandoning several possibilities, I eventually settled on the idea of exploring what John Wesley and his followers had to say about creation care. I tentatively titled my project "The Environmental Ethic of John Wesley and the Early Methodists," and I commenced my research in earnest.

I soon discovered two things that dampened my enthusiasm. First, Wesley and the early Methodists had very little to say about what we now call "environmentalism," as it simply was not part of eighteenth-century public dialogue. Further, it seemed to me that whatever little evidence there was of an environmental ethic in Wesley's thoughts and writings had already been thoroughly mined by others. There just didn't seem to be anything else to say.

But along the way I discovered something else that both fascinated and delighted me. Scattered throughout Wesley's sermons, letters, journals, books, and pamphlets—spanning his life and touching upon every aspect of his ministry—were repeated and passionate arguments and exhortations relating to food and ethical eating. I recognized themes in his thoughts and teachings that were very familiar to me.

Not long after enrolling in seminary I had stepped away from a busy and thriving law practice to return home to my family farm in Virginia. My wife and I decided to trade our professional urban lifestyles for a life spent raising goats, pigs, chickens, and organically grown vegetables. Inspired by writers and farmers like Wendell Berry, Michael Pollan, and Joel Salatin, we became full-time farmers, tending a small, chemical-free farm and trying to replicate for our customers and ourselves the food experience of a diversified family farm of a century ago. We had become producers in what is now loosely known as "the food movement," a phenomenon reflected in the surging interest throughout our culture in food produced naturally and sustainably.

To my surprise, in my research I found the same principles and ideals that were fueling this movement deeply embedded in the thoughts and teachings of John Wesley. Just as the food movement emphasizes the importance of nutritious food and a healthy diet, the humane treatment of animals, ethical food production, and opposition to overconsumption, so did John Wesley.

Despite being a lifelong Methodist, a student at a Wesleyan seminary, and now a full-time committed proponent of the food movement, I had never heard this before. As far as I could tell, Wesley simply was not a part of this conversation, even among the Methodists and Wesleyans at the forefront of the food movement. I discovered that, to the best of my knowledge, no one had ever comprehensively examined Wesley's food ethic, and certainly no one had ever made the connection between that ethic and our ongoing cultural conversation about food.

So I tossed out my work on Wesley's environmental ethics and started over, instead examining how Wesley's thoughts and teachings resonate with the guiding principles of the contemporary food movement. The thesis that emerged out of that work later evolved into this book. My hope is that it will help introduce a Wesleyan food ethic into the current conversation.

I am grateful to the many people who have provided me with invaluable help, inspiration, and guidance along the way. A few of them deserve special note. My thesis advisors at Asbury Theological Seminary were Dr. James Thobaben and Dr. Laurence Wood. My studies under Dr. Thobaben helped inspire the topic, and Dr. Wood was especially helpful in encouraging me to pursue publication of my work. Both of them offered advice and suggestions that have improved this book. I did not always accept their suggestions, however, so any remaining errors of fact or judgment are mine alone.

Without the help of my assistant (and friend) Valarie Taylor I'm not sure this book would have been possible. I am much obliged to her.

Finally, I am thankful for the support and encouragement of my wife and partner, Cherie, without whom this journey would never have begun.

Introduction

FOOD IS A hot topic these days. Over the past few years, interest in the sources and quality of our food has exploded. Farmers' markets, crowded with shoppers, are popping up all over the country in response to increasing demand for fresh, locally grown food. Organic food is the fastest-growing segment of the food market. A string of popular documentaries and best-selling books also attest to our culture's surging interest in food. Advocates of healthy and natural food have been propelled from virtual obscurity into celebrity status. There is even an organic garden at the White House.

"Americans today are having a national conversation about food and agriculture that it would have been impossible to imagine even a few short years ago," wrote Michael Pollan in his introduction to Wendell Berry's *Bringing It to the Table: On Farming and Food*.[1] This increasing cultural attention to food and food ethics is sometimes called the "food movement," and it has arisen, in large part, as a reaction to concerns generated by the modern industrialized food system. While people are drawn to this movement for a variety of reasons, there are some consistent themes. Advocates of the food movement:

- favor a diet of natural, whole, unprocessed foods, and attribute the increasingly troubling worldwide health crisis (particularly the obesity epidemic) to the industrial system's preference for processed and nonnutritious food,

- generally favor organically produced food over food produced in the chemical-based industrial system,
- generally oppose consuming meat, milk, and eggs from animals raised in "factory farm" concentrated animal feeding operations, preferring instead the products of animals raised more naturally, and
- prefer local community-based food economies, and generally disfavor the globalized industrialized food distribution system, complaining that it provides poorer quality food and is destructive of communities and the environment.

This book examines the intersection of the teachings of John Wesley with the ethics of the contemporary food movement, an intersection whose existence is generally unknown both to Wesley's spiritual and ecclesiological descendants and to the advocates of the contemporary food movement. So where is John Wesley in this conversation? What might an eighteenth-century English evangelist have to contribute to a twenty-first-century conversation about food? And why should anything he might have to say matter?

Within Wesley's work, there is an identifiable ethic deeply sympathetic to core arguments of the contemporary food movement. Wesley speaks directly and compellingly to the movement's emphasis on nutritious food, reasonable levels of consumption, and the humane treatment of farm animals. It is also possible to identify within Wesley's thoughts and work compelling arguments consistent with the food movement's preference for localized organic food production. If John Wesley were alive today, he would no doubt be a passionate and energetic ally of the food movement. And from his teachings, writings, and example, it is possible to discern and articulate a Wesleyan food ethic that can inform and benefit his spiritual descendants in today's food movement.

The book begins with a review of the contemporary food system—specifically, the rise of the industrial food system and the countervailing food movement it has generated. Then, after first briefly reviewing Wesley's life, and in particular those influences and events that shaped his food ethic, this book considers what his works reveal about his views on five of the principal themes of the contemporary food movement. These themes are:

- an insistence on nutritious food (and avoidance of food that is health-impairing),
- an advocacy of reasonable levels of consumption and avoidance of overeating,
- a desire for the humane treatment of farm animals,
- a preference for naturally raised, organic food, and
- a preference for localized community-based food production.

After examining where Wesley's teachings would locate him within the food movement (as well as the objections he might have to the movement), I will identify and suggest a specifically Wesleyan food ethic, relevant to our ongoing cultural conservation about food.

I expect many people will be surprised to discover how important food ethics were to John Wesley, and how central they once were to Wesleyan communities. My hope is that this Wesleyan food ethic will be rediscovered and returned to the place it once occupied in Wesleyan thought.

Organic
Wesley

1

The Rise of Industrial Agriculture and the Emergence of the Food Movement

[In America] diseases are indeed exceeding few; nor do they often occur, by reason of their continual exercise, and (till of late) universal temperance.

—JOHN WESLEY
A Primitive Physic, 1747

Today, one in three adults is considered clinically obese, along with one in five kids, and 24 million Americans are afflicted by type 2 diabetes, often caused by poor diet, with another 79 million people having pre-diabetes. Even gout, a painful form of arthritis once known as "the rich man's disease" for its associations with gluttony, now afflicts eight million Americans.

—MICHAEL MOSS
"The Extraordinary Science of Addictive Junk Food," 2013

TO UNDERSTAND AND appreciate how a Wesleyan food ethic might speak to our culture, we must first examine our prevailing food system. What are we eating? Why are we eating it? How is our food produced and distributed? What are the criticisms of the existing food system and why are they being made? As Wendell Berry famously put it, "Eating is an agricultural act." In order to best understand the issues we face when choosing our food, we need to have some basic understanding of our agricultural systems. So, to answer these questions, we will begin with a look at the current industrial food system and the countervailing food movement that has arisen in response to it. Although this story is told, in part, with statistics, try not to be put off by that. We will be returning to Mr. Wesley soon.

The Rise of Industrial Agriculture[1]

Agriculture seventy-five years ago was not much different from the agriculture of John Wesley's day. Most Americans lived on farms, where they tended gardens, saved seeds, and likely kept a milk cow, a few hogs, and a small flock of chickens. On farms such as these, families produced nearly all of their own food, usually also raising a cash crop to obtain the money needed to buy the things they were unable to produce for themselves. Food consumed in cities and urban communities came largely from the small farms in the surrounding rural areas.

In the years following World War II, however, American agriculture began to change dramatically, through what came to be known as the "green revolution." Increased mechanization decreased the necessity for human labor on farms and enabled farms to become ever larger. As mechanization increased, America's transition from a rural to an urban nation accelerated. Today, only about 15 percent of Americans live in rural areas, the lowest percentage ever. And these days few Americans raise or grow any of their own food. Whereas in 1945 approximately 30 percent of Americans were farmers and the average farm was 195 acres, today less than 1 percent of Americans claim farming as their occupation, and most cropland is on farms with more than 1,000 acres. Even among those Americans who still live in rural areas, 90 percent of them are not farmers. There are now twice as many Americans in prison as there are farming.

Over the past seventy-five years, mechanization, along with the use of pesticides, herbicides, and inorganic synthetic fertilizers, has caused crop yields to skyrocket. In 2013, for example, the average amount of corn produced per acre in America was twice that of just forty years earlier and more than four and a half times greater than the yield in 1945. Yields increased even more dramatically with the development of genetically modified seed. In the mid-1990s Monsanto Company introduced proprietary corn and soybean seeds whose DNA had been genetically modified to be resistant to its herbicide Roundup (glyphosate), thus enabling farmers to spray the herbicide directly on emerging crops, killing all vegetation but the crop plant. Monsanto also developed and introduced seeds genetically modified to include a pesticide in their DNA. Known as GMOs (genetically modified organisms) these crops rapidly came to dominate American agriculture. Virtually nonexistent before 1996, GMOs took agriculture by storm. By 2013, nearly all the soybeans, corn, and sugar beets grown in the United States were genetically modified. GMO products soon became ubiquitous in processed food. All told, 60 to 70 percent of the processed food sold in the United States contains at least one genetically modified ingredient.

These technological advances have also sharply reduced the number of farmers necessary to produce the crops. Today 89 percent of America's food production comes from fewer than 350,000 farmers (.001 percent of the population), a level of production that required more than 6 million farmers in the 1930s. According to the 2012 Census of Agriculture, 66 percent of U.S. agricultural output comes from a mere 4 percent of American farms.

The abundance of corn and soy resulting from the commodification and industrialization of agriculture has contributed to steep increases in the production of processed food, in which corn and soy by-products are usually primary ingredients. Generally speaking, processed foods are food items that could not be prepared in a household kitchen using the same ingredients, but rather require industrial techniques and chemical formulations and additives. Approximately 70 percent of the American diet is processed food, which is now cheap and abundant.

Just as industrialization and technological advances were changing vegetable and cereal grain production, animal-based agriculture was undergoing dramatic changes as well. Small-scale animal husbandry increasingly gave way to large industrialized concentrated animal feed operations (CAFOs), often referred to as "factory farms," which have essentially replaced the small family farm as the source of the nation's meat, milk, and eggs. In 1900, 95 percent of American farms had chickens; today less than 1 percent do. Likewise, 80 percent of American farms had milk cows, whereas today only 8 percent do, and nearly half of those are on farms with more than fifteen hundred cows and $1 million in annual sales.

The high-intensity CAFO structures on the factory farms have greatly reduced the amount of space necessary to raise animals, permitting farms to produce vastly more animals than they were able to raise when the animals lived outside and ranged pasture. Hogs are now commonly raised in large, industrial-scale, corporate-owned buildings, housing thousands of animals at a time. Egg-laying hens are kept in buildings that typically house about 125,000 birds each. Broilers (meat chickens) are also raised in concentrated indoor operations. A typical thirty-thousand-square-foot broiler production facility holds 37,000 to 46,000 chickens at a time, with well under one square foot of space allotted to each of them. A few decades ago it would take nearly four months for a chicken to reach slaughter size, but now, thanks to hybridization and specialized feed, they reach slaughter weight in only six to seven weeks.

The animals in the CAFOs are fed specially formulated feed, produced primarily from the GMO corn and soy grown on the large, industrialized, monocultural farms. To stimulate growth and to combat the disease that occurs in such concentrated confined operations, animals are also typically given low levels of antibiotics with their feed. Approximately 80 percent of the antibiotics used in the United States are fed to farm animals.

In the industrial system, beef cattle are taken off pasture and finished (raised to slaughter weight) in high-density feed lots, where they are given antibiotics and fed a diet of predominantly GMO corn and soy. Most beef cattle are also given hormonal growth promotants (HGPs), typically implanted in their ears, to stimulate rapid growth.

Dairy farms have also seen dramatic change. As recently as 1975 the average American dairy farm milked 25 cows. Today there are 135 cows on the average dairy farm (with large dairies typically having from 5,000 to 15,000 cows) and that number continues to rise. A mere 3 percent of American dairies now produce more than 50 percent of America's milk. Milk production has skyrocketed as well. In 1950 the average dairy cow produced about 5,300 pounds of milk per year. By 1965 production had increased to more than 8,300 pounds per cow. Today, amazingly, the average is close to 22,000 pounds of milk per cow, about four times more than the production of a generation earlier.

By employing these concentrated, high-intensity practices, and by integrating their operations with those of industrialized commodity agriculture, American animal-based agriculture has been able to produce meat, milk, and eggs in abundance, while keeping costs low. As one study summarizes it:

> Livestock farming has undergone a significant trans-formation in the past few decades. Production has shifted from smaller, family-owned farms to large farms that often have corporate contracts. Most meat and dairy products now are produced on large farms with single species buildings or open-air pens. Modern farms have also become much more effi-cient. Since 1960, milk production has doubled, meat production has tripled, and egg produc-tion has quadrupled. Improvements to animal breeding, mechanical innovations, and the intro-duction of specially formulated feeds and animal pharmaceuticals have all increased the efficiency and productivity of animal agriculture. It also takes much less time to raise a fully grown animal. For example, in 1920, a chicken took approximately 16 weeks to reach 2.2 lbs., whereas now they can reach 5 lbs. in 7 weeks.
>
> New technologies have allowed farmers to reduce costs, which mean bigger profits on less land and capital. The current agricultural system rewards larger farms with lower costs, which results

in greater profit and more incentive to increase farm size.[2]

The traditional diversified family farm is simply no longer representative of American agriculture. In the words of agricultural historian Paul Conkin:

> Narrowly specialized, large-scale farming departs widely from most images of the traditional family farm. In what sense does a 10,000-acre wheat farm in Kansas fit any definition of a family farm, when machines do all the planting and harvesting and the operator does not even live on the farm? Or what about a family-owned chicken farm with 20,000 broilers or 2,000 laying hens all housed in one-square-foot stacked cages in a large coop or barn, with no direct contact between the owner and the chickens? Or the 18,000 hog farmers who produce more than 90 percent of the total product, or the 11,000 beef cattle owners with annual sales over $1 million who market just over half our beef?[3]

Further, this highly specialized industrial food system is increasingly dominated by a handful of powerful multinational corporations. In his book *Deep Economy*, published in 2007, Bill McKibben reported,

> Four companies slaughter 81 percent of American beef. Cargill, Inc., controls 45 percent of the globe's grain trade, while its competitor Archer Daniels Midland controls another 30 percent. . . . Eighty-nine percent of American chickens are produced under contract to big companies, usually in broiler houses up to 500 feet long holding thirty thousand

or more birds. Four multinational companies control 70 percent of milk sales in the United States. . . . Five companies control 75 percent of the global seed market. . . . Walmart is now the largest seller of food in this country (and on the planet).[4]

The efficiencies of these large industrial operations enable them to operate on much smaller profit margins than small farms could afford, increasingly rendering small traditional family farms economically nonviable. McKibben reports, "Farmers' profit margins dropped from 35 percent in 1950 to 9 percent today. . . . To generate the same income as it did in 1950 a farm today would need to be roughly four times as large."[5]

As production has increased, so has the ability to distribute food quickly and over great distances. Gone are the days when a city's food needs would be met by the small farms surrounding that city. Now, with much of the formerly rural farming communities having been transformed into suburbs, there is a vast food distribution apparatus in place, which stocks American supermarket shelves with food originating on farms often thousands of miles away. This distribution network has rendered the seasonality of food largely irrelevant. In any town in America it is possible to buy produce without regard to whether it is in season locally: asparagus from Peru, blueberries from Costa Rica, and tomatoes from Mexico are common. Even when certain vegetables are in season in a particular area, the vegetables sold in that area's stores are usually not locally grown. On average, the food on an American plate these days has traveled fifteen hundred miles or more to get there.

Because of the distances involved and the time between harvest and consumption, traditionally favored heirloom vegetable varieties have been replaced with those varieties best suited for transportation, uniformity of appearance, and long shelf life. Likewise, traditional heritage breeds of farm animals have been replaced with those best suited to (and most profitable within) the factory farm/CAFO system.

This industrialization of agriculture has been welcomed as a means of liberating millions of Americans from the drudgery of farm life and has filled grocers' shelves with cheap and abundant food. Never in world history has food been as abundantly available, and at such low prices, as it is in America today. Americans spend on average less than 10 percent of their income on food, down from nearly 30 percent in 1950 and 17 percent only thirty years ago. Industrialized agriculture has made food shortages, at least in this country, a thing of the past.

Yet even as the industrialized food system has become more pervasive and more dominant, some have expressed opposition to its methods and consequences. The early critics were lonely voices, often dismissed as romantics or Luddites. The achievements of the industrialized food system, represented by steep increases in yields and supermarket shelves filled with an impressive variety of low-cost foods, were undeniable. The modern food system seemed to be personified in scientists, chemists, commodity traders, and biological engineers, rather than in a farmer and his mule. Objections to the booming industrial food system were written off as either nostalgic sentimentality, or as ignorance of the benefits of scientific progress.

The Emergence of the Food Movement

But over time a greater reaction to the dominant industrial system began to emerge, as a wider audience began to take more seriously the complaints being lodged against it. Among the critics and resistors were:

- people who preferred whole natural foods to processed foods,
- people who objected to the extensive use of chemicals, GMOs, and toxins on the industrialized farms,
- people who preferred supporting neighboring small farmers over buying their food from large corporations,
- people who preferred to obtain their meat, milk, and eggs from farms where the animals were pasture-raised using more traditional practices and without the extensive use of hormones and antibiotics,
- people concerned about the environmental damage done by industrial farming,
- people concerned about the adverse health conse-quences of eating food produced by the industrial system,
- people whose faith draws them to prefer food produced in more natural and traditional ways, and
- people who simply prefer the taste of fresh, traditional varieties of locally produced food.

What is the Food Movement?

This unorganized and multifaceted opposition to the industrial system is what I will call the "food movement." Sometimes called the "farm-to-table movement," the "local food movement," and the "organic" or "natural food movement," but most often not labeled as a movement at all, it is a phenomenon easily recognized in our culture, in everything from the rising popularity of farmers' markets to the proliferation of specialty, organic-themed grocery stores. It is reflected in our cultural groundswell of interest in food and the ethics of eating. Of course, this movement is not a formal organization per se, and most of its participants would not consider themselves part of a "movement." But whatever we call it, it exists and people are being increasingly drawn to it.

Because there is no single motive that animates those who are part of this movement, it resists precise definition. Those who fall under the food movement umbrella would include organic family-farmers, of course, but also backyard gardeners, foodies, locavores, patrons of farmers markets and specialty grocery stores (such as Whole Foods and Trader Joes), and everyone in between. They're a diverse lot, united by concerns over the quality of their food, the healthiness of their diets, and the ethical implications of their food choices. Whether their opposition is grounded in issues of personal health and well-being, the environment, animal welfare, public health, or some combination thereof, they generally oppose or, at the very least, are distrustful of the prevailing industrial food system. They are attracted to the food movement by a desire for food that is safe, nutritious, tasty, locally grown, and produced under humane and environmentally sensitive conditions, and by a corresponding belief that the industrial system does not produce such food.

Initially limited to a few marginalized health food advocates and early proponents of organic agriculture, over the past fifteen years or so the ranks of the movement have swelled; it has achieved mainstream acceptance, and its popularity is accelerating. Of course, there is nothing new about a desire for safe, tasty, nutritious, locally grown food. Farmers' markets have existed for as long as humans have been practicing agriculture, and since at least the time of Hippocrates we have understood that a good diet is essential to good health. And as recently as a couple of generations ago, of course, all food was organic. This food movement must be understood, therefore, not as something new, but rather as a reaction to the rise of the industrial food system and the damage it is perceived to have caused.

As this food movement has grown, organic agriculture and organic food have emerged as widely available alternatives to industrial agriculture and industrially produced food. Sales of organic food, defined as food produced without the use of pesticides, herbicides, synthetic fertilizers, genetically modified seed, antibiotics, or growth hormones, while still comprising only approximately 4 percent of the total food market, have nearly quintupled over the last ten years.

The rise of the food movement has also been accompanied by a steep increase in the popularity of locally produced food. The number of farmers' markets in America has increased by 76 percent since 2008, and direct sales from farmers to consumers have grown by more 700 percent since 2005.

Concern over the national health crisis that has followed in the wake of increased consumption of industrially produced food has also contributed to the rising popularity of the food movement. As the American diet changed from predominantly seasonal produce and locally raised meat to largely processed food, high in fats and sugars, an epidemic of obesity, diabetes, and related illnesses has followed. The rapid onset of widespread obesity is particularly shocking. According to the USDA, Americans consume nearly 500 calories per day more than they did in the 1970s, and those over age twenty are now nearly three times more likely to be obese than they were just thirty years ago.

Over the past three decades, childhood obesity has nearly tripled. The Centers for Disease Control warns that type 2 diabetes, which was until recently unknown in children and was commonly called "adult-onset" diabetes, is now a "sizable and growing problem among U.S. children and adolescents," for which the obesity epidemic may be "significantly responsible."

As Walter Willet, chair of the nutrition program at Harvard's School of Public Health, puts it,

> The transition of food to being an industrial product really has been a fundamental problem. First the actual processing has stripped away the nutritional value of the food. Most of the grains have been converted to starches. We have sugar in concentrated form, and many of the fats have been concentrated and then, worst of all, hydrogenated, which creates trans-fatty acids with very adverse effects on health.[6]

Writing in *New York Times Magazine*, Michael Moss noted,

> Today, one in three adults is considered clinically obese, along with one in five kids, and 24 million Americans are afflicted by type 2 diabetes, often caused by poor diet, with another 79 million people having pre-diabetes. Even gout, a painful form of arthritis once known as 'the rich man's disease' for its associations with gluttony, now afflicts eight million Americans.[7]

The shocking and dramatic rise in these diseases is linked directly to our diets, which have come to be dominated by unhealthy processed foods. In his book *Food Rules*, Michael Pollan wrote:

Populations that eat a so-called Western diet—generally defined as a diet consisting of lots of processed foods and meat, lots of added fat and sugar, lots of refined grains, lots of everything except vegetables, fruits, and whole grains—invariably suffer from high rates of the so-called Western diseases: obesity, type 2 diabetes, cardiovascular disease, and cancer. Virtually all of the obesity and type 2 diabetes, 80 percent of the cardiovascular disease, and more than a third of all cancers can be linked to this diet. Four of the top ten killers in America are chronic diseases linked to this diet.[8]

The CDC estimates that an amazing 75 percent of U.S. health care spending goes to treat chronic diseases linked to our diets.[9] Alarming statistics such as these have led many people to turn to the food movement in search of healthier, more nutritious food.

The food movement has also attracted those who oppose the industrial meat animal system, or factory farm CAFO system. Many within the food movement have elected to eat meat, if at all, only if it comes from animals raised in humane, traditional ways, and without the use of the growth hormones and antibiotics that are now common in industrial meat production. Thus, they prefer products from pasture-raised animals, such as grass-fed beef, pastured pork, and free-range chickens.

The growing popularity of the food movement is being reflected in popular culture as well. Best-selling books from authors such as Michael Pollan and Barbara Kingsolver promote nutritious, natural, and locally grown food, while drawing attention to the problems associated with industrial agriculture.[10] Poet, novelist, essayist, and farmer Wendell Berry has been producing critiques of the industrial food system for decades, until recently laboring largely in obscurity. These days he is rightly regarded as a principal founder of the food movement, and his work has begun to receive broad cultural acceptance and praise. In 2010, Berry was awarded the Presidential National Humanities Medal, and in 2012 he was selected to deliver the prestigious Jefferson Lecture for the Humanities, the highest honor the federal government confers for distinguished intellectual achievement in the humanities.

Documentaries such as *Food, Inc.* (2009), which received an Academy Award nomination for best documentary, have reached wide audiences. Virginia farmer Joel Salatin, a longtime outspoken advocate of the food movement and opponent of industrial agriculture, was featured in *Food, Inc.* and in Pollan's *The Omnivore's Dilemma*; and he has become a much sought-after speaker and a food-movement celebrity. First lady Michelle Obama has made the fight against childhood obesity one of her principal causes, and in 2009 she oversaw the creation of an organic garden on the White House grounds. In August 2014, the U.S. Postal Service introduced a special set of farmers' market stamps, declaring that "Farmers markets are an old idea that's new again." The Food Network, a cable television channel devoted entirely to food programming, is now a top-ten cable channel with more than one million viewers daily. Clearly, these days the food movement is vibrant, robust, and growing.

The Christian Response to the Movement

Although the food movement is predominantly secular, the values and ethics that have fueled its rise have resonated with Christians and within Christian communities.

Just as there is now broad Christian participation within the environmental movement, Christians are increasingly visible within the food movement as well. Some of its leading advocates, such as Joel Salatin and Wendell Berry, cite their Christian faith as an essential foundation of their beliefs. Motivated by an ethic of creation care, many Christians have come to see participation in the food movement as one way to be better stewards of creation. For many Christians, the choice of what to eat, and in what quantity, is not a morally or spiritually neutral decision.

Christians who have embraced the food movement often ground their participation in Scripture, citing obligations to tend and preserve the earth, to treat animals with compassion, to nourish and care for our bodies, and to help the poor and the hungry. For many believers, honoring and respecting creation is an essential part of honoring and respecting the Creator. They believe that eating well and maintaining good health contributes to a healthy overall relationship with God and with creation. Many also advocate local food systems as a way to invigorate and preserve local community-based economies and to help reduce the use of environmentally damaging fossil fuels. Numerous denominations and faith-based organizations have also joined in opposing the inhumane and unnatural treatment of animals in the CAFO system. Of course Christians have also been drawn to the movement by the deteriorating state of health in contemporary society, believing there is an obligation to God to tend properly and carefully to our bodies. The proliferation of church-based community gardens also has its roots in the food movement, and is often connected to efforts to deliver higher-quality, more nutritious food to the poor and food-insecure. The movement, and the broader call within the Christian community to an ethic of creation care, has been particularly attractive to younger evangelicals, seemingly put off by culture wars and more interested in finding ways to make a positive contribution to the world's well-being.

Unquestionably the food movement is vital and increasingly popular. It is now manifested across American culture, both secular and religious.

Now let us begin to look at the food ethics of John Wesley and how they speak to the motives and concerns driving the food movement. We will start with an overview of Wesley's life and ministry, focusing on the emergence of his food ethics.

For Discussion

1. In what ways has the food system changed over your lifetime? Have those changes improved our quality of life? Are there ways these changes have diminished our quality of life?

2. Think of your last few meals. Do you know where the food you ate was grown or raised? By whom it was raised? Do you know what ingredients the food contained? Were the meals eaten at home with your family? Were any of them eaten in your car?

3. Think of people you know who are healthy and fit. What kind of diet do they eat? Now think of people who are unhealthy and unfit. What is their general diet?

4. Think of a meal you ate at your grandparents' home when you were a child. How did it differ from typical meals of today? How did the food taste compared to your last family meal?

5. Are there ethical/moral issues associated with what and how we eat? What potential moral issues come to mind when you think about food?

2

John Wesley

He who governed the world before I was born shall take care of it when I am dead. My part is to improve the present moment.

—JOHN WESLEY
Letter to Mr. John Smith (Archbishop Thomas Secker),
March 25, 1747

Do good. Do all the good thou canst.

—JOHN WESLEY
"On Worldly Folly," 1790

JUST AS WE need to understand the context of our current food system to best appreciate how a Wesleyan food ethic might speak to it, it is likewise important to understand Wesley's food ethics in the overall context of his life and ministry. Before looking specifically at how his teachings on food and ethical eating intersect with the food issues faced by our culture, let us first begin with a review of Wesley's life and a consideration of the sources and origins of his teachings on food.

Wesley's Life and Legacy

John Wesley was the fifteenth of nineteen children born to Samuel and Susanna Wesley, nine of whom survived infancy. Born in 1703 in Epworth, England, Wesley grew up in a devoutly religious household. His father, Samuel, was a rector in the Church of England, and his mother was a stern disciplinarian who placed a particular emphasis on the religious instruction of her children. While not desperately poor, neither was the Wesley family wealthy. They lived a Spartan and sometimes meager existence, typical of the family of a rural cleric in that day.

Wesley attended Oxford University. While a student there he became fascinated with and attracted to the practices of the early Christian church. Along with his brother Charles, Wesley joined a group of students who felt a similar calling to austerity and piety, meeting regularly for prayer, devotions, and communion. This group, which came to be known derisively by its critics as "the Holy Club," practiced fasting every Wednesday and Friday until 3 p.m. (in imitation of the early church) and generally advocated a life devoted to Christian simplicity and holiness. Another name derisively applied to the group, which Wesley would eventually adopt, was "the Methodists."

Following his ordination, and after having been elected to a fellowship at the University, Wesley traveled to the American colony of Georgia, where he hoped to evangelize the Indians. While there Wesley became disillusioned as a missionary and was poorly received as a minister. After a failed romance, and to escape the legal proceedings that followed it, Wesley retreated to England, dejected.

On the voyage to America, Wesley had been deeply impressed by a group of German Moravians, whom he had seen praying and singing during a terrifying storm, apparently completely unconcerned about the danger. This left a lasting impression on him, and upon his return to England, Wesley sought out the Moravian community, seeking inspiration. In May 1738, at a Moravian gathering in London, Wesley had his famous Aldersgate experience, which he described as a feeling that his heart had been "strangely warmed." Shortly after having his zeal renewed, Wesley encountered the pastor George Whitefield, who had taken to preaching open-air sermons to the working classes. Eventually overcoming his initial resistance to this method of preaching (which ran afoul of his Anglican sensibilities), Wesley soon adopted the style himself, launching his career as an itinerant open-air preacher.

Although Wesley remained committed to the Church of England throughout his life, his methods and teachings were controversial and often put him at odds with the ecclesiological establishment. While always remaining respectful, Wesley demonstrated that he was not afraid of stepping on toes. In answer to a complaint that he had no authority to preach within another priest's parish, Wesley famously responded, "I look upon all the world as my parish."[1]

Wesley was energetic and tireless in his ministry. Wesley biographer William Abraham—"Wesley rode up to 20,000 miles a year on horseback. He preached 800 sermons a year to crowds as large as 20,000. In a typical day he was up at 4:00 a.m., he preached at 5:00 a.m., and he was on the road to his next assignment at 6:00 a.m."[2] By the time of his death in 1791 at age eighty-seven, Wesley had traveled more than 250,000 miles by horseback and preached more than 40,000 sermons, spearheading what came to be a Methodist revival in England.

While it was never Wesley's intent that his followers separate from the Anglican Church or create any new denomination, the Methodist Church arose to carry on his spiritual legacy following his death. Methodism was particularly popular in the newly established United States, spread by preachers Wesley had audaciously ordained, despite having no ecclesiastical authority to do so.

John Wesley left a deep mark on the history of the Christian faith. Today worldwide there are more than 75 million Christians in Methodist and Wesleyan denominations descended directly from Wesley's efforts. Additionally, there are nearly 300 million Pentecostals, whose roots are in the Methodist tradition.

"The Famous Dr. Cheyne"

It was while he was a student at Oxford that Wesley's studies led him to connect food and faith in significant ways. In 1724, Wesley read Dr. George Cheyne's *An Essay of Health and Long Life*, and it had a profound impact on him, deeply influencing his thinking for the remainder of his life. Cheyne was a physician from Bath and a medical celebrity in Wesley's day who had overcome morbid obesity and poor health with a regimen of exercise, proper sleep, and a temperate diet.[3] Cheyne attributed good health to practices he called "nonnaturals," so-called because they were rules of healthy living that he claimed originated with God and were contrary to the human impulse to overconsume and live intemperately. Cheyne placed a particular emphasis on nutritious diets. "A proper, well regulated and parsimonious . . . diet is the far greatest article of long life and health," Cheyne wrote in his 1740 book, *An Essay on Regimen*.[4]

Wesley enthusiastically embraced Cheyne's teachings and became a lifelong admirer of his work. Cheyne's call for temperance and dietary discipline resonated with Wesley, who along with his Methodist cohorts had already adopted the practice of twice-a-week fasting and other forms of self-denial that they believed were characteristics of the earliest Christian communities. Wesley immediately incorporated Cheyne's advice into his own personal practices, faithfully following Cheyne's recommendations for the rest of his life. Shortly after reading Cheyne's book, Wesley wrote his mother, saying, "I suppose you have seen the famous Dr. Cheyne's book of Health and Long Life . . . He refers almost everything to temperance and exercise and supports most things with physical reasons . . . In consequence of Dr. Cheyne I chose to eat sparingly and drink water." Wesley referred to Cheyne's *The Natural Method* as "one of the most ingenious books which I ever saw."[5] For the rest of his life Wesley credited his own good health in large part to having followed Cheyne's recommendations.

Wesley's Ministry— "Inward and Outward Health"

The emphasis of Wesley's teachings was always on spiritual renewal. He called his followers to a life of devotion, obedience to God, and holy living. But for Wesley spiritual improvement was never separated from physical well-being. Any assessment of Wesley's ministry is therefore incomplete if it does not take into account his concern for health and wellness.

Wesley believed people should seek to live a life free from physical illness. He understood any imperfections in humanity, whether physical or spiritual, to be consequences of humanity's fallen condition, and not part of God's original plan or ultimate purpose.

Wesley practiced and advocated a life of Christian discipline and self-control. He urged temperance, self-denial, and an avoidance of luxuries. He championed the practice of fasting, and complained that Christians practiced it too infrequently. In his sermons and other writings, Wesley regularly advocated healthy living as an essential part of a godly life. He promoted exercise and fitness, adequate sleep, proper medical attention, and most of all, a good diet. Indeed, from early in his life Wesley developed an appreciation of eating as a spiritual discipline. Wesley even attributed the origin of the term "Methodists" to ancient Roman physicians who taught that "all diseases might be cured by a specific method of diet and exercise."[6] Proper attention to health and wellness, for Wesley, was a vital component of proper devotion to God and essential to the message of the movement he founded.

Wesley's views derived from his holistic understanding of salvation. "Salvation," according to Wesley, "is not what is frequently understood by that word, the going to heaven, eternal happiness. . . . It is not a blessing which lies on the other side of death. . . . It is a present thing." As he said in a 1778 letter to Alexander Knox, "He wants to give you both inward and outward health."[7]

A Primitive Physic

Wesley devoted a substantial part of his life's work to improving the physical health and well-being of all people. To better serve the poor, who were unable to afford the services of physicians, for example, Wesley had resolved to "give them physic myself" and later wrote that he had for more than twenty-six years made "anatomy and physic the diversion of my leisure hours."[8] In 1747 he published *A Primitive Physic or an Easy and Natural Method of Curing Most Diseases*, a collection of folk remedies intended primarily to benefit the impoverished, who could not afford doctors, medicine, or medical books. For the title Wesley chose the word *Physic*, an archaic word meaning "medicine" or "health care" (the root of the word *physician*), because he was urging traditional "primitive" remedies.[9] Wesley's intended audience for the book was a society that rarely had any contact with a physician, and usually could not afford the services of one. *Primitive Physic* was wildly popular, going through thirty-two editions (twenty-three during his lifetime). It was one of the most widely read books in England between 1750 and 1850, and has been called one of the all-time medical best sellers.

Wesley made the book available for only a shilling, far less than comparable works sold for at the time, in the hope that it would be affordable to every family.[10] He advised the preachers under his authority to leave a copy of *Primitive Physic* in any home they visited. "It is a great pity that any Methodist should be without" a copy of it, Wesley wrote.[11]

Although many of the remedies in *Primitive Physic* appear quaint (or patently ridiculous) to modern readers, they tended to reflect the best scientific and medical knowledge of the day, and in many cases reflect holistic practices that are still followed.[12] Wesley's intent was to help inform people of inexpensive and natural remedies for illness, in keeping with his committed belief that there is a duty to do so. For the maintenance of good health, Wesley advised, above all else except prayer, exercise and a healthy diet.

Wesley's attention to health and physical well-being was not parallel to his interest in the soul and spiritual well-being, but rather was an integral part of it. He was convinced that God's original plan for humanity included healthy bodies and that we need not await the resurrection to start bringing our bodily health in line with God's plan. Wesley believed that God intends both "inward and outward healing" and that a properly oriented Christian life should promote both.

A Wesleyan Food Ethic?

Wesley published more than four hundred books and tracts during his lifetime, believing it was part of his calling. Within this abundant body of work, including sermons, treatises, tracts, letters, and journals, there is evidence from which we can discern where Wesley's views might locate him within the contemporary food movement, and from which we can identify the elements of a Wesleyan food ethic.

Proponents of the food movement, whether secular or religious, generally ground the ethics of the movement in five principal areas:

1. A desire for better health and more nutritious food
2. Advocacy of a moderate, reasonable level of consumption
3. Preference for natural farming practices over chemical-based farming (along with a concomitant desire to protect the environment)
4. A desire to avoid complicity in the abuse and mistreatment of farm animals
5. A preference for a food system that is local and sustainable rather than globalized and dependent upon industrialization

Let us now examine how Wesley's teachings might be relevant to each of these concerns.

For Discussion

1. What relevance does the work of John Wesley have in your faith community?

2. What are some of Wesley's most significant contributions to Christian thought, ethics, and theology?

3. What value might there be in studying Wesley's views and teachings on issues related to food and eating?

4. In our culture, what authorities do we look to for information and advice on issues of food ethics?

5. Do we tend to consider the views of the founders of our faith communities and denominations, or not? Should we?

3

Nutritious Food

Steadily observe both that kind and measure of food which experience shows to be most friendly to health and strength.

—JOHN WESLEY
A Primitive Physic, 1747

Eat food. Not too much. Mostly plants.

—MICHAEL POLLAN
In Defense of Food: An Eater's Manifesto, 2008

FOOD MATTERED IMMENSELY to John Wesley. Indeed, as odd as it may seem today, the importance of adhering to a nutritious diet was once at the very core of Wesleyan belief. Wesley taught that Christians have a moral duty to eat only nutritious food, and that there is a corresponding moral duty to refrain from eating food that is harmful to one's health. This was not some mere self-help afterthought for Wesley. Rather, it went to the very heart of his theology and it was a point of repeated emphasis throughout his life and ministry. Dietary discipline and attention to preservation of health was simply an essential part of being Wesleyan (or Methodist). These days, however, the food movement seems to be communicating that message far more effectively than Wesley's heirs.

A Life-or-Death Matter

First and foremost, the food movement is about promoting healthy, nutritious diets. Of course, there should be nothing remarkable about such a call to eat well. Indeed, there should be universal agreement that a diet of nutritious food is superior to a diet of nonnutritious food. In some sense, therefore, in urging a nutritious diet, and in criticizing unhealthy diets, the food movement merely states the obvious. The movement's advocacy of healthy food is not notable because it is innovative or novel, but rather because it stands in opposition to the prevailing industrial food system and because as a whole our society has chosen to eat poorly, notwithstanding the universal acknowledgment that doing so is injurious to health.

Thus the food movement urges a diet of nutritious foods, eaten in moderation. Among the proponents of the food movement there is a widespread belief that food produced naturally and without toxins and harmful chemicals is safer and more nutritious than the food produced by the chemical-dependent industrial system. While those claims may be debatable, there is no dispute that whole, natural foods are more nutritious than the sugary, fatty, starchy, highly processed foods that now compose about 70 percent of the American diet. Much of the energy of the food movement is therefore directed to promoting healthy diets of nutritious food and to discouraging the consumption of these processed foods.

In his book *In Defense of Food: An Eater's Manifesto*, Michael Pollan distinguishes "food" (meaning nutritious whole food) from processed food, which he refers to as "food-like substances." He boils his dietary advice down to seven words: "Eat food. Not too much. Mostly plants."[1]

In the face of a health crisis attributable to poor choices, proponents of the food movement argue that good nutrition is a matter of great urgency and should be made a personal and cultural priority. Pollan contends that the adverse health consequences of a diet of processed foods are reversible:

> People who get off the Western diet see dramatic improvements in their health. We have good research to suggest that the effects of the Western diet can be rolled back, and relatively quickly. In one analysis, a typical American population that departed even modestly from the Western diet (and lifestyle) could reduce its chances of getting coronary heart disease by 80 percent, its chances of type 2 diabetes by 90 percent, and its chances of colon cancer by 70 percent.[2]

Changing the standard American diet is therefore literally a matter of life or death.

Wesley's Emphasis on the Importance of a Nutritious Diet

John Wesley would wholeheartedly agree with the food movement's conclusions on the importance of a nutritious and wholesome diet. Throughout the decades of his ministry, Wesley consistently made nutrition and personal health a point of emphasis, never separating them from spiritual wellness. Always attentive to his own health and fitness, Wesley repeatedly emphasized to his followers the value of maintaining good health, stressing the role of eating nutritious food, exercising regularly, and appropriately protecting oneself from disease and sickness. Throughout his life he was particularly emphatic about the obligation to consume a healthful diet. For Wesley the quantity and quality of the food one eats is no small or trivial matter. Put simply, for Wesley, food mattered, and a nutritious diet had profound religious significance.

The Theological Foundations for Wesley's Food Ethic

Wesley never separated moral instruction from his teachings on diet, health, and wellness. Indeed, for Wesley, they were inseparable. To appreciate and understand Wesley's emphasis on a nutritious diet, therefore, it is necessary to understand the theological foundation upon which he grounded his beliefs. There are three principal reasons why Wesley placed such an emphasis upon good health and a nutritious diet.

1. Good Health Is God's Intent

First, Wesley was convinced that it is God's intent that all people be healthy. In Wesley's theological worldview, poor health is a reflection of the fallen, sinful state of the world, which God is presently in the process of redeeming and restoring to its intended goodness. Wesley taught and believed that people should strive toward the perfection (both physical and spiritual) that God intends. "We ought to preserve our health," he wrote, "as a good gift of God."[3] As Professor H. Newton Malony has noted, "Wesley took his cue from the biblical statement that 'the body is the temple of the Holy Spirit' (1 Corinthians 6:19), meaning that people's bodies were to be treated with great respect because they were like sacred buildings in which the spirit of God resided."[4] "Know you not that your body is, or ought to be, the temple of the Holy Ghost which is in you?" Wesley wrote.[5]

Further, Wesley was convinced that God "is already renewing the face of the earth," that all "infirmity and death" would someday end,[6] and that the new earth described in Revelation 21 was already in the process of being created.[7] So it follows naturally that we should strive to be and remain as healthy as possible, thus aligning ourselves more closely to God's will, while living into God's new creation.

2. Poor Health Diminishes a Person's Ability to Do Good for Others

Second, Wesley believed that poor health diminishes a person's ability to do good. For him, the human body was an instrument God intended to be used to do good, for the advancement and benefit of God's kingdom. Wesley argued that people are mere stewards of their bodies (like everything else they come to possess or control), which they are obliged to use to further God's purposes.[8] "Do all the good thou canst," he famously said.[9]

Because illness and debility can prevent a person from doing as much good as that person might otherwise be able to do, Wesley believed it was important to maintain and preserve health. Malony concludes, "According to Wesley . . . it was God's intention that humans fulfill their creative potentials through long and healthy lives. . . . Health was the means by which humans could do what God intended them to be and do."[10] Wesley was no doubt influenced in this regard by Cheyne, who wrote: "Without some degree of health, we can neither be agreeable to ourselves, nor useful to our friends; we can neither relish the blessings of divine Providence to us in life, nor acquit ourselves of our duties to our Maker, or to our neighbor."[11] For Wesley therefore, because an unhealthy body is less capable of doing good than a healthy body (a body "preserved in strength and vigour, a fit instrument for the soul," in his words) there is a moral duty to try to remain healthy, and a nutritious diet was essential to doing so.

3. Ruining Health with Poor Food Choices Is Self-Murder

Finally, and perhaps most significant, Wesley considered the intentional consumption of unhealthy food to be a form of suicide, and therefore sinful. Wesley interpreted the biblical commandment "Thou shalt not kill," as requiring that a person do nothing "hurtful to the health or life of your own body or any other's."[12] In commenting on the commandment, Wesley directed his argument specifically to food choices, pointedly asking the reader, "Are you guilty of no degree of self-murder? Do you never eat or drink anything because you like it, although you have reason to believe it is prejudicial to your health?"[13] Likewise, in a letter of April 16, 1777, Wesley wrote, "Thus our general rule is 'Thou shalt do no murder'; which plainly forbids everything that tends to impair health, and implies that we use every probable means of preserving or restoring it." Wesley was echoing Cheyne, who wrote in his *An Essay of Health*: "He that wantonly transgresseth the self-evident rules of health, is guilty of a degree of self-murder; and a habitual perseverance therein is direct suicide, and consequently the greatest crime he can commit against the Author of his being."[14]

Wesleyan theologian Rebekah Miles summarizes Wesley's position well:

> This is classic Wesley; a straightforward moral commandment not to kill is broadened, by way of his holistic model of holiness, into a commandment to avoid anything that would harm the health of one's own or another's body and an exhortation to do constantly that which is good for the body. This interpretation is a bit of a stretch, but Wesley was aware of the pastoral challenges and temptations of those to whom he was speaking or writing. The chances are good that the average person who happened to read Wesley's *Notes* in the eighteenth century would be in more immediate need of a word of admonishment about eating well than a reminder not to kill. It is likely that the same could be said today.[15]

The significance of Wesley's view on this cannot be overstated. Wesley was devoted to Scripture and grounded all of his teaching, ultimately, in his understanding of the Bible. Whatever practical benefits he may have believed would flow from a healthy diet, for Wesley the ultimate authority on the subject (as on any other) would be the Bible. By arguing that the divine commandment not to kill extends to doing nothing that would tend to harm one's own body, and that the commandment specifically prohibits the eating or drinking of anything that might be "prejudicial to health," Wesley was invoking his ultimate authority. For Wesley, eating health-impairing food "because you like it" was a form of "self-murder." Simply put, Wesley was convinced that knowingly consuming unhealthy food is a grievous sin.

"Didst thou use thy food . . . so as to preserve thy body in health?"

Wesley believed and taught that God expects food choices to be made with the preservation of health in mind, rather than the gratification of personal desires, and that those who choose to eat poorly will someday be required to account to their Creator for having done so. Indeed, Wesley went so far as to contend that on Judgment Day people will have to answer specifically for the wholesomeness of their diets. In his sermon "The Good Steward," Wesley described the scene: "The Lord of all will next inquire, 'How didst thou employ the worldly goods which I lodged in thy hands? Didst thou use thy food, not so as to seek or place thy happiness therein, but so as to preserve thy body in health, in strength and vigour, a fit instrument for the soul?'" Surely the prospect of answering such a question should be disquieting to those who have ruined their health with junk food and overeating.

There were those who objected to Wesley's emphasis on health and nutrition, arguing that, being a preacher, he should stick to "saving souls."[16] But Wesley rejected any attempt to dismiss physical well-being as being unimportant or unrelated to spiritual well-being. To the contrary, he taught and believed that personal holiness and obedience to God *required* careful attention to diet and health.

Wesley certainly had no patience with those who ate poorly simply because they enjoyed the taste of unhealthy food. "Prefer health before taste," he insisted. For Wesley, any pleasure (such as eating tasty but unhealthy food) that does not "spring from, and lead to, God" should be refused. Thus, he wrote, we must "refuse what we know to be deadly poison, though agreeable to the taste." Intentionally consuming such poison is sinful and a corruption of humanity's nature.

In summary, Wesley believed a diet of healthy, wholesome food is best suited to keeping the human body in the healthy condition he believed God desires and intends. A properly nourished body, healthy and fit, is most capable of doing the good works God expects from it. Eating a nourishing diet, he insisted, is a Christian obligation, while intentionally eating a diet of health-impairing food is a direct affront to God and a sin for which people will have to answer. In light of how strongly he held these beliefs, Wesley would find the contemporary church's relative silence on matters of nutrition and personal health distressing. Indeed, he might well be baffled at a contemporary Christian culture that calls itself pro-life while engaged so pervasively in "self-murder."

For Discussion

1. Do you find Wesley's reasons for eating a healthy diet convincing? Why or why not?

2. Have you ever heard a sermon on the theological importance of a healthy diet? Do you think pastors and religious leaders are putting an emphasis on the importance of a healthy diet? If not, why do you think that is the case?

3. Have you observed any changes in the overall health of your community over the past thirty years? Are those changes related to diet? If so, in what way?

4. Does the American church share in the responsibility for the poor diets and overconsumption that seem to be characteristic of today's society?

5. How might John Wesley's teachings on these issues be helpful to American Christians suffering from the effects of a poor diet?

4

Eating in Moderation

As to the quantity of their food, good sort of men do not usually eat to excess. . . . And provided they take only that measure of plain, cheap, wholesome food, which most promotes health both of body and mind, there will be no cause of blame.

—JOHN WESLEY
"The More Excellent Way," 1787

Americans on average now eat nearly 2,600 calories a day, almost 500 more than they did forty years ago, according to the USDA. . . . The two food groups Americans are eating more and more of—added fats and oils, and flour and cereal products—are the same ones that are found in most processed and fast foods.

—ROBERTO FERDMAN
"How the American Diet Has Failed," 2014

IN 1744 BENJAMIN Kennicott (who would later become a well-known cleric and biblical scholar) went to see John Wesley preach. He recorded his impressions of the controversial evangelist and his description of Wesley is both striking and telling: "He is neither tall nor fat; for the latter would ill become a Methodist."[1] As Kennicott's joke reveals, in Wesley's day obesity and Methodism were seen as inconsistent. Aversion to overeating was so characteristic of the early Methodist movement that one would no more expect to encounter an obese Methodist than a drunken one. Indeed, from the beginning, dietary discipline and moderation in eating were fundamental components of the Wesleyan food ethic.

The Obesity Epidemic

At the time he wrote *Primitive Physic*, Wesley was able to say of America, "There diseases are indeed exceeding few; nor do they often occur, by reason of their continual exercise, and (till of late) universal temperance." Things have certainly changed. Today nearly 70 percent of Americans are overweight, and more than one-third are clinically obese.[2] Continual exercise and universal temperance are certainly not traits anyone would consider to be characteristic of Americans these days.

The adverse health consequences of a diet rich in highly processed foods are most evident in the obesity epidemic that has swept across America over the last twenty-five years. The facts are shocking. Data collected by the Centers for Disease Control and Prevention (CDC) reveal that whereas as recently as 1996 no state had an obesity rate of more than 20 percent, by 2010, a mere fourteen years later, *every* state in America had an obesity rate greater than 20 percent, and in twelve states the obesity rate exceeded 30 percent. Over the last thirty years, obesity rates among children have doubled, and among adolescents they have tripled. Overall, more than 35 percent of American men and women are now obese, as are almost 17 percent of American children and adolescents. Americans today are nearly three times more likely to be obese than they were a mere three decades ago.

Obesity increases the risk of heart disease, stroke, type 2 diabetes, and certain types of cancer. The CDC estimates that medical expenses attributable to obesity exceed $147 billion per year (by comparison, the United Nations estimates that the amount needed to end world hunger is $30 billion per year, about one-fifth of what we spend annually treating obesity-related illnesses). On average an obese person spends nearly $1,500 per year more on health care than does a person of normal weight, a cost that is often transferred to society as a whole. According to the American Society of Clinical Oncology, obesity is now poised to overtake tobacco use as the nation's leading preventable cause of cancer. One study has concluded that nearly one-fifth of all deaths in America each year are linked to obesity.[3]

A complex set of factors contribute to the obesity epidemic, and obesity can sometimes be linked to genetics, environmental conditions, and cultural influences. At its root, however, is an increase in caloric intake that has occurred as we have transitioned to diets composed

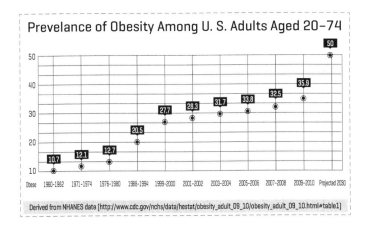

Prevelance of Obesity Among U. S. Adults Aged 20–74

Derived from NHANES data [http://www.cdc.gov/nchs/data/hestat/obesity_adult_09_10/obesity_adult_09_10.html#table1]

predominantly of unhealthy processed foods. According to the USDA, Americans today consume on average nearly 500 more calories per day than they did forty years ago, with the increased calories coming almost entirely from oil, fats, and grains. So-called fast food, which is high in calories and low in nutritional value, now accounts for more than 13 percent of Americans' diets, up from only about 3 percent in 1978.

Wesley and the Obesity Epidemic

We can be sure that Wesley would be highly critical of a society experiencing an obesity epidemic, as diets leading to obesity violate all of his teachings and beliefs about food, proper nutrition, and dietary discipline. Obesity tends to destroy the health of the body. It diminishes life span, leads to an increased reliance on pharmaceuticals and medical care, and tends to initiate serious life-threatening illnesses, such as cancer, diabetes, and coronary disease.[4] As with any other condition that impairs health, Wesley would see obesity and its resulting adverse health consequences as damaging and impairing bodies that God intends to be healthy and fit. Wesley would also object that obesity diminishes a person's ability to do good, in that it reduces mobility and endurance, leading often to debility and dependence. Perhaps most importantly, Wesley would likely see the obesity epidemic, at least in part, as a consequence of moral failure, conflicting with his emphasis on the virtues of temperance, dietary discipline, and self-control. Undoubtedly Wesley would join with the food movement in condemning the standard contemporary diet that has spawned this epidemic.

"They know how much they have sinned by excess of food."

Obesity was not unknown in Wesley's day, although it was certainly rare in comparison to contemporary society. Wesley estimated that 90 percent of the English people adhered to a diet of "plain and simple" food, eating only "what nature requires, and no more."[5] Indeed, malnutrition in Wesley's day would far more likely have been manifested in infirmities caused by eating too little food, rather than too much food. Obesity would therefore have been a condition found almost exclusively among the sedentary rich. Because of heavy drinking and a rich, gluttonous diet, George Cheyne, for example, grew to weigh more than 350 pounds before adopting the lifestyle changes advocated in his book *An Essay on Health and Long Life*.

Wesley would therefore have understood the adverse health consequences of overeating, or of eating obesity-inducing, unhealthy food, to be primarily products of gluttony, an absence of self-control, indulgences resulting from personal pleasure-seeking and therefore inconsistent with personal holiness and devotion to God. Indeed, Wesley specifically characterized eating "excess food" as sin and a transgression of "the holy law of God" that is harmful not only to the health of the body but also to the soul: "Many of those who now fear God are deeply sensible how often they have sinned against him, by the abuse of these lawful things," he wrote. "They know how much they have sinned by excess of food; how long they have transgressed the holy law of God, with regard to temperance, if not sobriety too; how they have indulged their sensual appetites, perhaps to the impairing even their bodily health,—certainly to the no small hurt of their soul."[6]

Overcoming this kind of sinful behavior, "the abuse of lawful things," was a point of emphasis in Wesley's teachings. He was pleased to list among the accomplishments of Methodism that "very many of the common people among whom they preach . . . were gluttons or drunkards, and are now temperate."[7]

Wesley was, of course, a firm believer in the practice of fasting. Throughout his ministry he championed the discipline, often complaining that Christians practiced it too infrequently. "A man that never fasts," Wesley declared, "is no more in the way to heaven than the man that never prays." For Wesley, the avoidance of "excess" was "a perpetual reason for fasting." Those who have chosen to fast for this reason, he said, "keep at a distance from all excess. . . . They often wholly refrain; always taking care to be sparing and temperate in all things." By choosing to fast in this way, "Every wise man . . . will wean (his soul) more and more from all those indulgences of the inferior appetites, which naturally tend to chain it down to earth, and to pollute as well as debase it."

For Wesley, temperance (meaning moderation in all consumption) was a primary virtue, and overconsumption, particularly overeating, was a moral failure. In his sermon "The More Excellent Way" Wesley wrote, "As to the quantity of their food, good sort of men do not usually eat to excess. . . . And provided they take only that measure of plain, cheap, wholesome food, which most promotes health both of body and mind, there will be no cause of blame." Likewise, in his essay "The Character of a Methodist," Wesley said that a Methodist cannot "fare sumptuously every day," alluding to the story of the rich man and Lazarus from Luke 16. In that story, a rich man who, during his life, "fared sumptuously every day," suffered in torment in Hades after his death. "Whoever thou art that sharest in the sin of this rich man," Wesley wrote, "were it no other than 'faring sumptuously every day,' thou shalt as surely be a sharer in his punishment, except thou repent, as if thou wert already crying for a drop of water to cool thy tongue!"[8]

"Are you temperate in all things? . . . Do you eat no more at each meal than is necessary?"

Wesley urged his Methodist preachers to always eat a little less than they desired, a practice he personally followed throughout his life.[9] "Take no more food than nature requires," he wrote in his 1784 treatise "Thoughts on Nervous Disorders." At age sixty-eight, reflecting on the reasons for his lasting health, Wesley identified his lifelong moderate eating as the key.[10]

Temperance in eating was an essential component of Wesley's call for personal discipline. He consistently taught that Christians should practice "self-denial," avoiding all luxuries, unnecessary expense, and overindulgence in food and drink. Such self-denial, in Wesley's view, was an essential part of proper Christian living.[11]

Wesley was fond of quoting Thomas à Kempis: "The more thou deniest thyself, the more thou wilt grow in grace,"[12] and he identified temperance in food as a "prudential means of grace." Thus Wesley called upon Christians to ask themselves, "Are you temperate in all things? For instance in food: Do you use only that kind and degree which is best both for body and soul? Do you see the necessity of this? . . . Do you eat no more at each meal than is necessary?"[13] If Wesley asked those questions of Christians today, it is safe to say he would not be pleased with most of the answers he received.

Wesley often criticized the eating of unhealthy food, particularly to excess, as intemperance inconsistent with personal holiness. In his essay "A Plain Account of Christian Perfection," Wesley described the shortcomings of those who had not attained Christian perfection, writing, "Some are wanting in temperance. They do not steadily use that kind and degree of food which they know, or might know, would most conduce to the health, strength and vigour of the body." Thus Wesley equated "temperance" (perhaps his favorite virtue) with eating a quantity and quality of food that is most conducive to health and strength, and he found fault both with those who know their diet does not promote health and those who "might know."

Indeed, Wesley considered "temperance in food" to be specific evidence of "the fruit of the Spirit."[14] In his December 10, 1748, "Letter to a Friend Concerning Tea," he wrote, "Though the kingdom of God does not consist in 'eats and drinks,' yet, without exact temperance in these, we cannot have either 'righteousness or peace or joy in the Holy Ghost'!" Wesley urged that people "use as little and plain food, exercise as much self-denial herein at all times, as your bodily strength will bear."[15] He was famous for his own self-discipline and he expected it from anyone else who was serious about Christianity.

"The costly and delicate food you eat, you are snatching from the mouths of the hungry."

Wesley condemned gluttony and overconsumption not only out of a belief that intemperance conflicts with personal holiness, but also out of a concern for social justice and the needs of the poor. For him, overeating reflected selfish personal devotion to one's own pleasure, rather than to the needs of others. He regarded spending money on more food than one needs to maintain health to be a diversion of resources that should properly go to the needy.

Wesley pulled no punches when challenging Christians who filled themselves to excess while others went hungry. "The costly and delicate food which you eat," he wrote, "you are snatching from the mouths of the hungry."[16] He further advised, "And in order to enlarge your ability of doing good, renounce all superfluities. Cut off all unnecessary expense in food, in furniture, in apparel. Be a good steward of every gift of God, even of these his lowest gifts."[17] Likewise, in his treatise "A Farther Appeal to Men of Reason and Religion" Wesley wrote, "By this needless and continual expense, you disable yourself from doing good. . . . You might have fed the hungry . . . ; but the superfluities of your own table swallowed up that whereby they should have profited." No doubt Wesley would continue to be critical of those who overeat to the point of obesity, while others remain hungry.

Moreover, we now know that overconsumption hurts the poor not just by taking food off their plates (as Wesley recognized), but also by diverting limited medical resources to the treatment of obesity-induced

illnesses. These resources might otherwise be spent
on health care for individuals suffering from illnesses
not caused by their own voluntary (and poor) choices.
Further, the poor in developing countries tend to suffer
the consequences of environmental degradation caused,
in part, by overconsumption in affluent countries.[18]
And as our industrialized food system increasingly
exports American junk food to the developing world,
obesity rates (and the illnesses associated with obesity)
are skyrocketing in places it was previously unknown.[19]
Because Wesleyan ethics always stand in opposition to
any behavior by the privileged that tends to harm the
poor, a Wesleyan food ethic would necessarily stand in
opposition to overconsumption and diets of obesity-
inducing food.

Overfed and Undernourished

Further, and importantly, the contemporary obesity
epidemic is not a consequence solely of gluttony and
overconsumption. Whereas in Wesley's time (as in
much of the world today) malnutrition was evidenced
by emaciation, in our society malnutrition is much more
likely to be evidenced by obesity. Alarming numbers
of Americans these days are both overfed and under-
nourished as a result of diets that are calorie-rich and
nutrient-poor. Factors that contribute to obesity among
the poor include a lack of access to nutritious food, an
inability to afford such food, and a lack of education
and awareness of the consequences of eating processed
food. Of course the fact that the obesity epidemic is
in some part attributable to social injustices (such as
the existence of "food deserts" and a relative lack of

access to nutritious food) should only serve to increase a Wesleyan passion for challenging the prevailing industrial food system.

"He is neither tall nor fat; for the latter would ill become a Methodist."

Despite Wesley's lifetime of teaching on this issue, such that in the eighteenth century one might joke that being obese would "ill become a Methodist," today, in the midst of the obesity epidemic, there is evidence that Methodists are likelier to be obese than the general public, and that Methodist pastors are even likelier to be obese than their congregants. These days the jokes are liable to be like Garrison Keillor's: "You know you are a Methodist when doughnuts are a line item on the budget."[20] No doubt this would deeply trouble Wesley.

According to a 2010 study published in the journal *Obesity*, the rate of obesity among Methodist pastors in North Carolina is more than 10 percent higher than that of the general population:

> North Carolina's United Methodist clergy have higher rates of diabetes, arthritis, high blood pressure, angina and asthma than do comparable people in the state. . . . Much of the reason for declining clergy health is related to their increasing waistlines: Nearly 40 percent of North Carolina's United Methodist clergy are obese, a designation given to individuals who have a body mass index (BMI) of 30 or higher. By comparison, the average North Carolinian in the study fares much better— only 29 percent of North Carolinians are obese.

Furthermore, only 25 percent of clergy, and 30 percent of North Carolinians, are of normal weight: that is, neither overweight nor obese.[21]

Put differently, three-fourths of the Methodist clergy in North Carolina are overweight or clinically obese.

Of course this is not a problem limited to Methodists; pastors in other denominations are also likelier than the general public to be obese. The same *Obesity* article cites, for example, a 2002 study by the Evangelical Lutheran Church reporting that 34 percent of ELCA pastors were obese, compared to the then national average of 22 percent. Anecdotally, in his book *The Rest of Life*, Ben Witherington describes speaking to a convention of Southern Baptist pastors and their wives and being shocked to see that "a considerable majority of them were overweight" and that more than 30 percent of them were "certifiably obese or morbidly obese."[22]

Overeating: The Accepted Vice

Although the obesity epidemic (and the adverse health consequences that come with it) has affected the entire country, it is particularly severe in the South and among rural communities.[23] Interestingly, those areas with the greatest rates of obesity are also those areas with the highest rates of church attendance. In a 2006 study of the relationship between obesity and religion, Purdue University sociologist Ken Ferraro concluded, "America is becoming known as a nation of gluttony and obesity and churches are a feeding ground for the problem. . . . Overeating is not considered a great sin—it has become the accepted vice."[24] A 2011 study by researchers at Northwestern University based on research conducted over eighteen years, found that people who attend church services at least once a week are a stunning 50 percent more likely to become obese than those who do not.[25] These facts surely might reasonably suggest that too little is being done by churches to combat obesity in their communities, congregations, and pulpits.

We can be sure that John Wesley would be shocked and appalled at the health crisis that poor diets and over-eating has produced. He would be critical of those who overconsume at the expense of others and at the cost of their own health. Obesity's adverse effect on human health would alone be more than enough to draw Wesley to the food movement's campaign against it. Moreover, his advocacy of the virtue of temperance, and his corre-sponding belief that intemperance (such as overeating and overconsumption generally) is harmful to the poor, would of course serve to intensify his motivation to chal-lenge the values and morals of a society overeating to the point of rampant obesity.

Of course, we now know that there are a complex set of reasons for the obesity epidemic and that reducing them to "gluttony, intemperance and an absence of self-control" would be overly simplistic and too narrowly judgmental. Some of those who are obese have genetic or physical infirmities that have contributed to their obesity. Many more are victims of a food system in which poor food is often the cheapest and most convenient. We should expect that Wesley would recognize the web of reasons for the obesity epidemic and not judge all of its victims to be gluttons. Nevertheless, we should also expect that he would continue to insist on temperance, self-control, and dietary discipline as a means of preventing and reversing the epidemic.

"The Power of Exercise"

Wesley believed and taught that good health requires not only a nutritious diet and self-control, but also proper amounts of physical exercise. Any review of his teachings on personal health would be incomplete if it did not take into consideration his strong views on the importance and necessity of exercise.

Wesley recognized the connection between over-eating and physical inactivity, arguing that overeating leads to laziness. "Luxury is constantly the parent of sloth. Every glutton will, in due time, be a drone. The more of meat and drink he devours, the less taste will he have for labour," he wrote in his 1775 sermon "National Sins and Miseries." Wesley thus recognized that a person's diet should take into account his or her amount of exercise, and that those who are not physically active should eat less than those who are. In *A Primitive Physic* Wesley wrote "for studious persons, about 8 ounces of animal food, and 12 of vegetable, in 24 hours, is sufficient."[26] He lifted this advice directly from Cheyne's *An Essay on Good Health*, while leaving out Cheyne's further recommendation of "about a pint of wine, or other generous liquor."[27]

Wesley himself was an active and physically fit man and was throughout his life an ardent advocate of exercise and physical fitness.[28] A biographer described him as "thin but muscular, and without superfluous flesh."[29] He stood five foot three and weighed only about 122 pounds, a weight he maintained constantly throughout his adult life.[30]

Wesley began a regimen of daily exercise as a child, and never abandoned it, remaining fit well into his old age. Writing in his journal at age eighty-five he attributed his continuing good health to, among other things, "my constant exercise and change of air."[31] After walking from Kingswood to Bristol, at the age of eighty-five, Wesley wrote of his friends who complained that he had done so, "It seemed so sad a thing to walk four or five miles! I am ashamed that a Methodist preacher, in tolerable health, should make any difficulty of this."[32]

Without exercise, Wesley insisted, "the human body can no more continue in health than without sleep or food," and he recommended a minimum of an hour of exercise, at least twice a day.[33] In *A Primitive Physic* Wesley wrote, "the power of exercise, both to preserve and restore health, is greater than can well be conceived; especially in those who add temperance thereto, who . . . steadily observe both that kind and measure of food which experience shows to be most friendly to health and strength."[34]

Wesley insisted that "a due degree of exercise is indispensably necessary to health and long life."[35] "Exercise, especially as the spring comes on, will be of greater service to your health than a hundred medicines," he wrote in a letter dated February 23, 1767.[36] This advice was typical of Wesley. In a letter to Alexander Knox dated January 28, 1780, he wrote, "I cannot advise you in the meantime to shut yourself up at home; it is neither good for your body nor your mind. You cannot possibly have bodily health without daily exercise in the open air; and you have no reason to expect the spirit of a healthful mind unless you use the means that God has ordained."[37] Likewise, in a letter to Samuel Bradburne dated June 16, 1781, Wesley wrote, "The more exercise he uses, winter or summer, the more health he will have." With exercise and "a strictly temperate diet," Wesley argued, "few chronical diseases will stay long."[38]

"Vice does not lose its nature, though it becomes ever so fashionable."

Undoubtedly if Wesley were alive today, he would continue to insist on the importance of temperance, which he defined as eating only that "kind and degree" of food that is most conducive to health, and we can expect that he would particularly insist that Christians have a duty to practice temperance and moderation in their food choices. Certainly Wesley would not be sympathetic to an argument that culture has changed, so overconsumption and self-induced obesity should no longer be considered immoral. As he wrote in "The Character of a Methodist," "Vice does not lose its nature, though it becomes ever so fashionable."[39]

Advocacy of a healthy diet of nutritious food, eaten in moderation, is a consistent theme both of the food movement and of the ministry of John Wesley. Proponents of the food movement argue that a diet of healthful foods promotes physical well-being, while a diet of unhealthy, processed foods promotes illness and obesity. Clearly Wesley would share and embrace this view. No doubt he would be horrified by the obesity epidemic, and especially so at its prevalence among Christians. For Wesley to join with the food movement in challenging and opposing the industrial food system while championing a diet of nutritious food, eaten in moderation, would be simply to continue a persistent and central theme of his ministry.

For Discussion

1. Have you seen evidence of the obesity epidemic in your own family? In your church? In your community? What do you think are the reasons for the dramatic increase in obesity in our society?

2. What do you think a Christian response to the obesity epidemic should be? How can Christians best address the obesity epidemic, without shaming or condemning those who are victims of it?

3. What is your church community doing to address the obesity problem? Have any of the Wesleyan teachings described in this chapter ever been discussed in your church? Should they be?

4. What would John Wesley think of the food served at church functions these days?

5. What effect might the increase in childhood obesity have on our culture long-term? What kinds of food are given to children at church functions in your church? How might the church best lead in trying to reverse the childhood obesity epidemic?

6. Do you perceive people to be less physically active these days than they were in the past? What role do you think insufficient exercise plays in the obesity epidemic? What is an appropriate Christian response?

5

Farm Animals

Animal factories make an economic virtue of heartlessness toward domestic animals, to which humans owe instead a large debt of respect and gratitude.

—WENDELL BERRY
"Stupidity in Concentration," 2002

Let them extend in its measure the rule of doing as they would be done by, to every animal whatsoever.

—JOHN WESLEY
"On the Education of Children," 1783

WATCHING BULLDOGS ATTACK and fight an enraged tethered bull was a popular community pastime in Wesley's day. Not only did spectators find this practice (known as "bull-baiting") amusing; it was commonly believed that baiting a bull both improved the taste of its meat and also made it safer by thinning the bull's blood, which was otherwise believed to be poisonous. In fact, some English towns had laws prohibiting the sale of any meat from a bull that had not first been baited.

Notwithstanding these beliefs, Wesley decried bull-baiting as inhumane and unchristian. "It is not needful to say anything more of these foul remains of Gothic barbarity," Wesley wrote, "than that they are a reproach, not only to all religion, but even to human nature."

His criticism was not well received. William Windham, the minister of war in Pitt's government, when defending the practice of bull-baiting, complained that Methodists wanted to prohibit "everything joyous . . . to prepare the people for the reception of their fanatical doctrines."[1] Bull-baiting was not outlawed in England until 1835.[2]

Wesley and the early Methodists insisted that Christians have a duty to treat animals humanely and with compassion. This attention to animal welfare, which Windham dismissed as a fanatical doctrine, was an important component of Wesleyan teaching and ethics. In the case of bull-baiting, the Methodist concern for animal welfare came into conflict with a popular and prevailing method of preparing farm animals for human consumption. Perhaps it still does.

Industrial-Scale Animal Production

The contemporary food movement urges diets that are primarily vegetable-based, and opposes the industrial factory farm method of raising farm animals. Those who identify with the food movement argue that if meat is not avoided altogether, only nutritious meat should be eaten, in moderation, and from animals raised naturally and humanely.

By employing factory-style, concentrated animal feed operations (CAFOs), industrial agriculture has been able to increase production of meat, eggs, and milk dramatically, while at the same time creating economic efficiencies that keep its products cheap and its profits high. As mentioned in chapter 1, since 1960, milk production has doubled, meat production has tripled, and egg production has quadrupled.[3] But these gains in production have come with a price. CAFO practices bear little resemblance to the animal husbandry traditionally practiced on family farms. Daniel Imhoff, in the introduction to the 2010 book *The CAFO Reader: The Tragedy of Industrial Animal Factories*, wrote:

> As the name implies, a CAFO is a feeding operation. Animal density and weight gain are the primary objectives. These animal factories are quite different from small- or medium-size diversified farms that combine row or tree crops with livestock raised on pastures, using the animals' manure to fertilize the fields or orchards. Most CAFOs shouldn't really even be described as farms—either technically or legally—because they basically operate under an industrial factory framework. In a CAFO, animals are concentrated in unnaturally high stocking rates by the thousands or tens of thousands and under unnatural conditions, often unable to breathe fresh air, see the light of day, walk outside, peck at plants or insects, scratch the earth, or eat a blade of grass. They are fed a high-calorie grain-based diet (sometimes including reclaimed animal manure, ground-up fish, or recycled animal parts) designed to maximize growth and weight gain in the shortest amount of time. Only a select few modern breeds are chosen for these cold industrial parameters.[4]

Nearly 10 billion chickens, pigs, and cows are now slaughtered in American each year, double the number in 1980 and ten times the number in 1940.[5] And again, whereas hogs and chickens were traditionally raised outside on pasture, in their natural environments, now the vast majority of them are raised inside buildings housing thousands of animals at a time. Likewise, in the prevailing industrial model, beef and dairy cattle are also raised in enormous concentrated feeding operations. Beef cattle are taken off pasture and finished in massive feedlots, where they are fattened using hormonal growth promotant implants (HGPs) and diets of genetically modified grain. Large dairy operations now milk thousands of cows per day, many of which have been given a hormone that boosts milk production. Most of the pigs raised in industrial agriculture operations are treated with ractopamine, a porcine growth hormone. To speed up growth, and to keep them healthy, animals in CAFOs are routinely fed antibiotics.

Increasingly, those who look carefully at these factory farm operations are objecting to them. Consider biblical scholar Sandra Richter's description of hog CAFOs:

> Factory farming is the practice of raising livestock in confinement at high-stocking density, where the farm operates essentially as a factory whose end product is protein units. Confined animals burn fewer calories, their excrement is mass-managed (or mismanaged as many argue), and their fertility and gestation fully controlled. As regards America's most lucrative agricultural product, pigs, confinement has been distilled into an exact science: twenty 230 lb. animals per 7.5 square-foot pen, housed upon metal-grated flooring, in climate controlled conditions, who are never actually exposed to the light of day. These animals are sustained in such crowded and filthy conditions that movement is difficult, natural behaviors impossible, and antibiotics are essential to the control of infection. Sows (typically a 500 lb. creature) are separately housed, living out their lives in 7-foot by 22-inch metal gestation crates from which they are never released,

even in the process of giving birth. They are artificially inseminated to deliver an average of eight
litters, litters inflated beyond their natural carrying
capacity by fertility drugs.[6]

Pigs are physiologically similar to humans, and they
have advanced cognitive abilities (causing them to be
perceived as intelligent).[7] By nature they forage for food
by rooting in the earth. They establish an area for their
waste, and will not defecate near where they sleep or
nurse their young. When a sow is nearing the time to
deliver her piglets, she builds a nest in a safe, dry place.
Pigs that spend their entire adult lives on slatted concrete
floors in cages seven feet long and twenty-two inches
wide, however, are denied the ability to act on these
instincts. Forced to stand in their own feces and deprived
of the room even to turn around, they gnaw at the bars
of their cages, driven mad by the inability to nest before
farrowing.[8] In a 2012 press conference, a spokesman for
the National Pork Producers Council responded to criticism of these practices by saying, "So our animals can't
turn around for the 2.5 years that they are in the stalls
producing piglets. . . . I don't know who asked the sow if
she wanted to turn around."[9]

Nor is life any better for hens in industrial egg operations. To get the millions of layers they need, the industry
artificially inseminates eggs, then hatches them in enormous incubators. The day-old chicks are then placed
on a conveyor belt and sorted by sex. The male chicks
are tossed alive into giant meat grinders (or thrown into
large containers to die more slowly). About 200 million
chicks are killed this way in the United States every year.
After being debeaked (because hens in battery cages
will sometimes peck at the hens in adjoining cages),

the day-old hens are transported in crates to massive brooding facilities until they are large enough to begin laying eggs. Then they are placed inside cages in long rows, stacked on top of one another. The hens are fed the cheapest feed that will enable them to produce the most eggs in the shortest time. They never see sunlight, an insect, a blade of grass, or any living thing other than one another and the unfortunate people who work in these facilities. They never stretch their wings, take a dust bath, roost, scratch in the dirt, hatch an egg, brood their young, or see a rooster. Their entire seventy-week adult life is spent on a piece of wire mesh slightly smaller than a standard piece of paper.[10] Then, once their egg production begins to drop, the hens who have survived this life are killed and made into soup, pet food or, in some places, into chicken feed.

"The Father of All has a tender regard for even his lowest creatures."

Throughout his life John Wesley had a high regard for the animal kingdom. He consistently opposed all forms of animal cruelty, teaching that we have a moral obligation to be compassionate and humane in our treatment of animals. We are to see God in the eye of every creature, Wesley insisted, continuing, "We should use and look upon nothing as separate from God, which indeed is a kind of practical atheism."[11] This understanding of the inherent holiness and worth of all creatures informed Wesley's consistent advocacy for humane treatment of animals. "I doubt not that the Father of All has a tender regard for even his lowest creatures," he declared in his famous sermon "A General Deliverance."

Wesley spent much of his life on horseback, and his insistence that horses be properly treated is well-known. Wesley advised his preachers, "Be merciful to your beast. Not only ride moderately, but see with your own eyes that your horse be rubbed, fed and bedded."[12] Wesley's concern for animals, however, extended far beyond just those upon whom he depended for transportation.

In a society where animals were commonly abused for sport, Wesley was a zealous activist for the elimination of such practices. Thus, Wesley and his Methodist movement attacked such things as bull-baiting, dogfighting, and cock-fighting. This opposition was so persistent, frequent, and well-known that it became common in eighteenth-century England to ridicule anyone who opposed cockfighting as being "a Methodist."[13] Critics of Wesley's Methodist movement complained that Methodists "took away from the pitman his gun, his dog and his fighting cock."[14]

"Let them extend in its measure the rule of doing as they would be done by, to every animal whatsoever."

While Wesley certainly objected to the frivolity of sports oriented around the abuse of animals, his objection extended more broadly to a general concern for the welfare of the animals. For example, Wesley instructed parents to teach their children to be compassionate to animals and to do nothing that would needlessly harm or cause pain to any animal, even going so far as to extend the golden rule to them:

> But truly affectionate parents will not indulge (children) in any kind or degree of unmercifulness....

They will not allow them to hurt, or give pain to,
anything that has life. They will not permit them to
rob birds' nests; much less to kill anything without
necessity, —not even snakes, which are as innocent
as worms, or toads, which, notwithstanding their
ugliness, and the ill name they lie under, have been
proved over and over to be as harmless as flies. Let
them extend in its measure the rule of doing as they
would be done by, to every animal whatsoever.[15]

By standing in opposition to the mistreatment
of animals, Wesley put himself at odds not only with
popular opinion, but also with the scientific and intellectual establishment of his time. In Wesley's day, and
arguably in ours as well, the prevailing scientific view was
that animals do not experience pain in the way humans
do, and that any human concern for animal welfare was
mere sentimentality. In his book *Discourse on Method*,
Rene Descartes had put forth and popularized the argument that, unlike humans, animals are only "machines"
and "automata." Proponents of this view argued that
since animals, being mere machines, do not feel pain, it is
therefore not possible to be cruel to them. In the words
of Nicolas Malebranche: "They eat without pleasure,
cry without pain, grow without knowing it; they desire
nothing, fear nothing, know nothing."[16]

Wesley emphatically rejected this so-called Cartesian
view, insisting instead that animals have feelings, and
should be treated with compassion and respect. In his
Survey of the Wisdom of God in the Creation, Wesley
responded at length to the argument of "several eminent
men" that animals are "mere machines," for whose care
and welfare humans need not be concerned. "Do we not
continually observe in the brutes [a now-archaic word for

animals] which are round about us a degree of reason?"
Wesley asked. Further, he argued:

> Were it true that brutes were mere machines, they
> could have no perception of pleasure or pain. But
> how contrary is this, to the doleful significations
> they give, when beaten or tormented. How contrary
> to the common sense of mankind—For do we not all
> naturally pity them, apprehending them to feel pain
> just as we do, whereas no man is troubled to see a
> plant torn, or cut, or mangled how you please? And
> how contrary to scripture, "A righteous man regar-
> deth the life of his beast: but the tender mercies
> of the wicked are cruel." Prov. xii. 10. The former
> clause is usually rendered a good man is merciful to
> his beast. And this is the true rendering, as appears
> by the opposite clause, that the wicked is cruel.
> Cruelty then may be exercised toward beasts. But
> this could not be, were they mere machines.
>
> The natural instinct of all creatures, and the
> special provision made for some of the most help-
> less, do in a particular manner demonstrate the
> great Creator's care.[17]

Wesley thus rejected any suggestion that animals are
mere machines, undeserving of compassion. Instead he
insisted that while it is impossible to be cruel to a machine
or a plant, common sense shows that animals feel pain
just as we do. For Wesley, common sense revealed that it
is possible to be cruel to animals, and Scripture prohibits
such cruelty.

Wesley stood, therefore, in opposition to the
prevailing views of his day: that the only consideration
due to animals was to determine how they might best

be used to amuse or benefit humans. Rather, he believed and taught that the animals and the rest of the natural world had intrinsic value, independent of any use that humans might have for them.[18] He rejected his culture's claim that animals are machines incapable of suffering, as nonsensical and unchristian. Do unto animals, Wesley said, as you would have animals do unto you.

Treat Animals Well, in Anticipation of God's New Creation

Wesley's regard for the proper treatment of animals was not mere sentimentality. Rather, his beliefs were solidly grounded in his theology. God loves and cares for animals, he argued, and therefore so should we. We ought to "imitate Him whose mercy is over all his works," Wesley declared.[19]

Just as Wesley believed that we should seek to maintain and preserve physical health in anticipation of the new creation to come, so likewise did he believe that we should respect animal life in anticipation of the restoration of God's "peaceable kingdom." Indeed, taking care of human bodies and respecting animal life were both integral to Wesley's understanding of salvation.

Wesley took the biblical story of Eden seriously, and literally. He believed that before the fall all creatures lived in harmony with one another and there was no predation. All animals—including humans—were vegetarian. This is the nature of creation as God originally intended it, he taught, and therefore it is also the nature of the world as it will ultimately be, once fully redeemed and restored by God.

> Indeed, such is the miserably disordered state of the world at present, that innumerable creatures

can no otherwise preserve their own lives than by destroying others. But in the beginning it was not so. The paradisiacal earth afforded a sufficiency of food for all its inhabitants; so that none of them had any need or temptation to prey upon the other. The spider was then as harmless as the fly, and did not then lie in wait for blood. The weakest of them crept securely over the earth, or spread their gilded wings in the air, that wavered in the breeze, and glittered in the sun, without any to make them afraid. . . . There were no birds or beasts of prey; none that destroyed or molested another; but all the creatures breathed, in their several kinds, the benevolence of their great Creator.[20]

Wesley's views on the treatment of animals were consistently informed by this belief that human cruelty to animals is an effect of the introduction of sin into the world, and that in their natural, God-intended states, both animals and people were gentle, kind, nonviolent, and not carnivorous. Once God has fully redeemed and restored creation, he insisted in his sermon "The New Creation", this peaceful, nonviolent, non-predatory state of conditions will return:

On the new earth, no creature will kill, or hurt, or give pain to any other. The scorpion will have no poisonous sting; the adder, no venomous teeth. The lion will have no claws to tear the lamb; no teeth to grind his flesh and bones. Nay, no creature, no beast, bird, or fish, will have any inclination to hurt any other; for cruelty will be far away, and savageness and fierceness be forgotten. So that violence shall be heard no more, neither wasting or destruction seen on the face of the earth. "The wolf shall dwell with

the lamb," (the words may be literally as well as figu-
ratively understood) "and the leopard shall lie down
with the kid: They shall not hurt or destroy," from the
rising up of the sun, to the going down of the same.

The General Deliverance

Wesley was thus confident that God's ultimate plan
of salvation and redemption extends to all of creation,
including animals. He ultimately detailed his eschatological vision in his remarkable sermon "The General
Deliverance," published in 1871. In this sermon, Wesley
considered the state of animals before the fall, in the
present, and upon the full restoration of creation.

In the original order of creation, Wesley argued,
animals were not only immortal; they were also rational
and enjoyed an existence of pure pleasure, beauty, and
goodness. The violence now inherent among animals
occurs only as a result of sin having entered into the
world, corrupting creation. But, he contended, whereas
much of the violence animals inflict upon each other
in the natural world is a result of their need to survive,
human mistreatment of animals is not a necessity, and
is therefore worse. "What a dreadful difference there is
between what they suffer from their fellow brutes and
what they suffer from the tyrant, man!" Wesley wrote.
"The lion, the tiger, the shark, give them pain from mere
necessity, in order to prolong their own life; and put them
out of their pain at once. But the human shark, without
any such necessity, torments them of his free choice; and
perhaps continues their lingering pain till after months or
years death signs their release."

Wesley taught and believed that in God's restored
new creation, which animals will share with humanity,

animals will return to their original beauty, peacefulness, and understanding. All violence in the animal world will end. In his words, "No rage will be found in any creature, no fierceness, no cruelty, or thirst for blood."

Wesley noted how animals suffer in our world, but argued that they too will someday have a reward and a deliverance:

> Thus, in that day, all the vanity to which they are now helplessly subject will be abolished; they will suffer no more, either from within or without; the days of their groaning are ended. At the same time, there can be no reasonable doubt, but all the horridness of their appearance, and all the deformity of their aspect, will vanish away, and be exchanged for their primeval beauty. And with their beauty their happiness will return; to which there can then be no obstruction. As there will be nothing within, so there will be nothing without, to give them any uneasiness: No heat or cold, no storm or tempest, but one perennial spring. In the new earth, as well as in the new heavens, there will be nothing to give pain, but everything that the wisdom and goodness of God can create to give happiness. As a recompense for what they once suffered, while under the "bondage of corruption," when God has "renewed the face of the earth," and their corruptible body has put on incorruption, they shall enjoy happiness suited to their state, without alloy, without interruption, and without end.

Wesley was convinced that God would not have permitted the fall only to restore creation eventually to the condition that existed before it. Rather, he believed that God will ultimately redeem and restore creation to a condition *even better* than that which existed before the fall. "May I be permitted to mention here a conjecture concerning the brute creation? What, if it should then please the all-wise, the all-gracious Creator to raise them higher in the scale of beings?" he wondered. "What, if it should please him, when he makes us 'equal to angels,' to make them what we are now, creatures capable of God; capable of knowing and loving and enjoying the Author of their being?" Perhaps, Wesley speculated, when all of creation is restored and redeemed, animals will have the faculties of speech, reason, and understanding that humans now have.[21]

Anticipating an objection that it is of no value to speculate about such things, Wesley offered two responses. First, for Wesley this was not just idle and fanciful theological speculation. Rather, it was fundamental to his theodicy. Starting, as he did, with the proposition that there was no suffering among animals in the original creation, and observing the magnitude of suffering among the animal kingdom now, Wesley wondered why animals should be so severely punished for sins they did not commit. Imagining that God would someday compensate them for their undeserved suffering, by elevating their status beyond even that which they originally occupied before the fall, helped Wesley come to terms with the problem of evil in the animal kingdom. He thus defended his speculation, saying:

> May it not answer another end; namely, furnish us
> with a full answer to a plausible objection against
> the justice of God, in suffering numberless creatures
> that never had sinned to be so severely punished.
> They could not sin, for they were not moral agents.
> Yet how severely do they suffer!—yea, many of

them, beasts of burden in particular, almost the whole time of their abode on earth; So that they can have no retribution here below. But the objection vanishes away, if we consider that something better remains after death for these poor creatures also; that these, likewise, shall one day be delivered from this bondage of corruption, and shall then receive an ample amends for all their present sufferings.

Secondly, beyond the value his speculation had for theodicy, Wesley defended it on practical grounds as well:

One more excellent end may undoubtedly be answered by the preceding considerations. They may encourage us to imitate Him whose mercy is over all his works. They may soften our hearts towards the meaner creatures, knowing that the Lord careth for them. It may enlarge our hearts towards those poor creatures, to reflect that, as vile as they appear in our eyes, not one of them is forgotten in the sight of our Father which is in heaven. Through all the vanity to which they are now subjected, let us look to what God hath prepared for them. Yea, let us habituate ourselves to look forward, beyond this present scene of bondage, to the happy time when they will be delivered therefrom into the liberty of the children of God.

Wesley's views on animal salvation had been long held. It seems that as early as his days at Oxford, Wesley believed that animals have souls and some capacity for reason. Although the text is now lost, it is known that one of Wesley's three disputation lectures for his master's degree at Oxford in 1727 was on the souls and reasoning powers of animals.[22]

Thus, Wesley saw that treating animals with compassion and respect serves not only to help make the existing world a place that better reflects God's intent for it, but it is also a way to participate in the in-breaking of the new creation. As Wesley scholar Randy Maddox put it, Wesley "frequently exhorted against abusive treatment of animals. Avoiding such abuse ourselves, and helping prevent it by others, was one way he made clear in which we can cooperantly allow God's work of cosmic new creation to impinge upon the present."[23]

Wesley thus believed that both animals and humans are to be final beneficiaries of God's grace and salvation, and any consideration of Wesley's views on the treatment of animals must remain mindful of that fact. This belief informed his conclusion that Christians have a moral obligation to treat animals with compassion and respect.

Wesley on Vegetarianism

Wesley's insistence upon humane and ethical treatment of animals did not, however, extend so far as to require a strictly vegetarian diet. Although Wesley kept to a vegetarian diet at times during his life, and counseled others to do the same, he never contended that vegetarianism is a religious obligation. Indeed, on several occasions he specifically rejected that notion. In his essay "The Character of a Methodist," Wesley wrote, "Our religion does not lie in . . . abstaining from . . . meats and drinks, which are all good if received with thanksgiving." Likewise, in a letter to the bishop of London dated June 11, 1747, Wesley wrote specifically that "Christianity does not require . . . abstaining from wine and animal food."

Indeed, Wesley once temporarily abandoned his own vegetarian diet, even though he felt it had improved his health, out of a concern that his vegetarianism might be perceived as a religious practice. In his letter to the bishop of London, he explained:

> By "extraordinary strictnesses and severities," I presume your Lordship means the abstaining from wine and animal food; which, it is sure, Christianity does not require. But if you do, I fear your Lordship is not thoroughly informed of the matter of fact. I began to do this about twelve years ago, when I had no thought of "annoying parochial ministers," or of "captivating" any "people" thereby, unless it were the Chicasaw or Choctaw Indians. But I resumed the use of them both, about two years after, for the sake of some who thought I made it a point of conscience; telling them, "I will eat flesh while the world standeth" rather than "make my brother to offend." Dr. Cheyne advised me to leave them off again, assuring me, "Till you do, you will never be free from fevers." And since I have taken his advice, I have been free (blessed be God) from all bodily disorders.

Some of Wesley's attraction to vegetarianism can be attributed to his admiration for the early Christian community, and his belief that they ate no meat. While at Oxford, Wesley was influenced by Claude Fleury's book *Manners of Early Christians*, which claimed that the early Christians were vegetarians and drank no wine. Wesley eventually published his own abridged version of Fleury's book, in which he recommended abstaining from "drinking wine or eating flesh."[24]

Though he did not consider it a religious obligation, however, Wesley was convinced that a meat-free diet was most conducive to good health. Indeed, Wesley always insisted that he was never healthier than during the times he refrained from eating meat.[25]

Wesley therefore taught that diets should be vegetable-based and that if meat is eaten at all, it should be consumed in moderation. In his sermon "On the Education of Children," Wesley advised mothers to "accustom [their children] to the most simple food, chiefly of vegetables." In his 1784 treatise "Thoughts on Nervous Disorders," Wesley identified the overconsumption of meat as damaging to the nerves. Throughout his life and ministry Wesley consistently advised that, for health reasons, no meat should be eaten at the evening meal. "Eat no flesh at supper, but something light and easy of digestion," he advised.[26] For those who do not eat only "bread or herb of the field," Wesley insisted that they should nevertheless limit themselves to "the kind and measure of food which experience shows to be most friendly to health and strength."[27]

Thus, while Wesley insisted that Christians have a moral obligation to treat animals humanely and compassionately, he did not claim that they have a moral obligation to refrain entirely from eating meat. He did, however, insist that a healthy diet (which he identified as a Christian obligation) should include little meat. Just as meat-eaters in today's food movement do, Wesley could reconcile those positions by avoiding eating the meat of animals that were raised in inhumane conditions.

Wesley's Views on Eating Animals Raised Unnaturally

One of the food movement's principal objections to industrial animal agriculture is that animals raised in confinement are denied the opportunity to forage and enjoy natural, varied diets. Animals raised in CAFOs are fed a diet composed primarily of feed made from corn and soybeans. Pigs and chickens are omnivores, and so while a diet of grain may be less wholesome than a diet that includes natural foraging, and may result in inferior meat and eggs, such a diet is not necessarily damaging to the health of the animal.[28] Cattle, on the other hand, are ruminants, physiologically adapted to a diet of grass, not grains, and a grain-based diet is damaging to their health.[29] In either event, for all animals raised in CAFOs, natural diets and foraging are replaced with unnatural industrial feeding systems.

Proponents of the food movement object to the industrial method of raising animals on unnatural diets and therefore favor products from animals raised on pasture. So, for example, they prefer eggs and meat from free range or pastured poultry, the eggs and meat of chickens raised outdoors on pasture being markedly different from those of chickens raised inside in confinement, both in taste and nutritional value.[30] Likewise, proponents of the food movement favor beef and dairy products from grass-fed cattle, rather than from animals fed grain in high-intensity operations. Grass-fed beef has a distinctive taste, and is generally preferred by proponents of the food movement, who also contend that the meat is more nutritious than that of animals finished on grain.[31]

As there were no CAFOs in Wesley's day, we might not expect to find any evidence as to which side Wesley would take in this debate. Interestingly, however, Wesley's mentor Dr. George Cheyne spoke out directly in opposition to the eighteenth-century equivalent of these practices, arguing that the meat produced using such practices was less healthy for humans to eat, and Wesley expressed sympathy with his view.

In his 1733 book *The English Malady*, Cheyne wrote:

Instead of the plain simplicity of leaving the animals to range and feed in their proper element, with their natural nourishment, they are physicked [medicated] almost out of their lives and made as great epicures as those feeding on them, and by stalling, cramming, bleeding, laming, sweating, purging, and thrusting down such unnatural and high seasoned foods into them, these nervous diseases are produced in the animals themselves even before they are admitted as food to those who complain of such disorders. Add to all of this the torturing and lingering way of taking away the lives of some of them to make them more delicious and the dressing of them by culinary torments while alive, for their purchaser's table; all which must necessarily sharpen, impoison, corrupt and putrify their natural juices and substances.[32]

It is remarkable how closely Cheyne's criticism tracks with contemporary objections to CAFO practices—that animals are taken out of their natural element, denied their natural diets, given unnatural foods and excessive medicines, tortured for the benefit of the ultimate purchaser, all resulting in food that is less nutritious than that from animals naturally raised. In his book *An Essay on Health and Long Life*, Cheyne argued specifically that meat from grass-fed animals is the most nutritious, and he objected to eating "stall fed beef and mutton" and "crammed poultry."[33] (Cramming poultry was the practice of inserting food into the mouths of the birds with a type of funnel, for the purpose of fattening them more quickly and, presumably, producing more desirable meat.)[34]

In his discussion of how nutritious meat should be produced, Cheyne used language that could just as easily have come from someone in today's food movement: "The only way of having sound and healthful animal food is to leave them to their own natural liberty, in the free air, and their own proper element, with plenty of food, and due cleanness, and a shelter from the injuries of the weather, when they have a mind to retire to it."[35] Indeed, Cheyne's language is strikingly similar to that of Wendell Berry from nearly three hundred years later: "Though I am by no means a vegetarian, I dislike the thought that some animal has been made miserable in order to feed me. If I am going to eat meat, I want it to be from an animal that has lived a pleasant, uncrowded life outdoors, on bountiful pasture, with good water nearby and trees for shade."[36]

Shortly after first reading Cheyne, Wesley wrote his mother, with excitement, specifically expressing his approval of Cheyne's condemnation of stall-fed beef:

> I suppose you have seen the famous Dr. Cheyne's book of *Health and Long Life* . . . He refers almost everything to temperance and exercise and supports most things with physical reasons . . . He entirely condemns eating anything salty or highly seasoned, as also pork, fish, and *stall-fed cattle* and also recommends for drink two pints of water and one of wine in twenty-four hours . . . in consequence of Dr. Cheyne I chose to eat sparingly and drink water.[37]

Given Wesley's admiration for Cheyne's work, how faithfully he followed Cheyne's advice, and how consistently he recommended Cheyne's practices for the rest of his life, there is every reason to believe that Wesley would join with Cheyne, and therefore with the contemporary food movement, in opposing the eating of meat from animals raised in confinement, on medicines and unnatural diets.

Wesley on Industrial Meat

Thus Wesley would likely join the food movement's opposition to factory-farm CAFOs, on the grounds both that the facilities are unnatural and inhumane, and that the CAFO-produced products are not as nutritious as those of animals raised on pasture. Likewise, Wesley would concur fully with food movement guru Michael Pollan's advice to eat mostly plants. No doubt if Wesley were alive today he would advise that meat, even from animals raised humanely and ethically, should be eaten sparingly.

Wesley would not look at a hen in a battery cage, a sow in a gestation crate, or a steer in a feedlot, and see mere machines, which should be converted into human food as cheaply, efficiently, and quickly as possible. Rather, he would see creatures loved by God ("not one of them is forgotten in the sight of our Father which is in heaven"), destined to be included and rewarded in God's redeemed and restored creation, and toward whom Christians should show compassion and respect. A man who preached the importance of kindness and mercy to horses, snakes, and toads would certainly feel no less compassion for pigs, cows, and chickens. Wesley's theology would inform his assessment of factory farming and the CAFO system, and leaves little doubt that he would condemn it. Given the choice between meat from the industrial system or animals raised on the farms favored by the food movement, we can be certain that Wesley would prefer the latter.

For Discussion

1. These days few of us ever see the animals we eat while they are still alive. How might our attitudes toward eating meat and the treatment of farm animals change if we had to raise and slaughter the animals ourselves?

2. Do Christians have a moral obligation to refrain from abusing animals? Does that obligation extend to animals raised to be our food? Should we take it into account when choosing what to eat?

3. Do you find Wesley's insistence that animals be treated with compassion convincing? How should humans treat animals, particularly those raised to be our food?

4. Have you ever heard a sermon that contains any of the teachings from Wesley found in this chapter? If not, why do you suppose these teachings have been lost?

5. Do you intend to make any changes to your diet based on what you've read in this chapter? Why or why not?

6

Organics, Processed Food, and Chemical-Based Farming

They introduced into practice . . . chemicals such as (the common people) had neither skill, nor fortune, nor time to prepare; yea, and of dangerous ones, such as they could not use, without hazarding life, but with the advice of a physician.

—JOHN WESLEY
A Primitive Physic, 1747

All of creation is an object lesson of spiritual truth. So what does a farm that illustrates compassion, holiness, forgiveness, abundance, faith, and order look like? . . . I would suggest that a farm that builds soil, heightens immunological function, produces more nutrient density, and runs on real-time sunshine more consistently illustrates divine attributes than one that destroys soil, produces deficient food, runs on petroleum, and reduces immunological function.

—JOEL SALATIN
Interview, RedLetterChristians.org, 2014

THE FOOD MOVEMENT favors food that is produced organically. Farmers who grow their crops organically (whether they seek USDA certification or not) may vary in their practices, but common to them all is a refusal to use GMOs, synthetic pesticides, herbicides, and synthetic fertilizers. Animals raised organically are given no growth hormones, and have access to pasture at all times. As with the food movement generally, those who favor organically produced food typically do so because they believe it to be tastier, more nutritious, less dangerous, and more ethically produced. (Of course, not all of these factors will be important to every consumer, nor will all consumers weight them the same.)

Would Wesley Eat Organic?

John Wesley ate nothing but organic food. Farming practices in Wesley's day were little changed from those of the previous two thousand years. There were no pesticides, no herbicides, no fungicides, no synthetic inorganic fertilizers, no genetically modified seed, no CAFOs, and no use of growth hormones and antibiotics in animal husbandry. Wesley, like everyone else in his world, ate organic food because it was the only kind of food that existed.

What would Wesley think about the food movement's insistence on food produced without the use of herbicides, pesticides, hormones, antibiotics, genetic modifications and synthetic fertilizers? If he were alive today, would Wesley eat organic? Would he counsel his followers to do so?

As shown earlier, Wesley was a passionate advocate of nutritious diets, and an equally passionate critic of the practice of eating unhealthy food. If Wesley believed food produced organically to be more nutritious than food that was not, then almost certainly he would be an advocate of an organic diet. Likewise, if Wesley concluded that there was something unethical (or, to choose the word he would more likely use, "sinful") about the way nonorganic food is raised or grown, then he could be expected to oppose eating it, and to advocate an organic diet instead.

The USDA defines organic food as food

> produced by farmers who emphasize the use of renewable resources and the conservation of soil and water to enhance environmental quality for future generations. Organic meat, poultry, eggs, and dairy products come from animals that are given no antibiotics or growth hormones. Organic food is produced without using most conventional pesticides; fertilizers made with synthetic ingredients or sewage sludge; bioengineering; or ionizing radiation.

While many proponents of organic food tout its health advantages and insist it is more nutritious than food produced conventionally, the evidence used to support that claim is disputed. For example, although a 2012 study at Stanford University concluded that there were no significant nutritional differences between organic food and conventional food, a 2014 study published in the *British Journal of Nutrition* by a team of international researchers concluded that organic food has substantially higher levels of antioxidants and substantially lower levels of toxic metals and pesticides than conventionally grown food.[1] On whether organic food is more nutritious, the Mayo Clinic concludes, "Probably not, but the answer isn't yet clear."[2] Wesley would certainly favor organic food if its health advantages were indisputable. Because they are not, however, the matter is not so easily settled, and some deeper digging is required.

The concept of "organic food" was unknown in Wesley's day. There being no discussion of organic and industrial food, Wesley never had any occasion to speak to the matter. Therefore, to determine what conclusion

Wesley would likely reach, it is necessary to reason by analogy.

Despite the obvious lack of any direct references to the subject, there are very good reasons to believe Wesley's food ethics would incline him toward food that is organically produced.

1. Wesley's Preference for the Natural over the Synthetic

Within Wesley's work and thought there is a decided preference for "natural organic cures" over synthetic, or chemical ones.[3] "Medicines will do you little service," he wrote. "You need only proper diet, exact regularity, and constant exercise, with the blessing of God." In fact, Wesley urged, one should combine these with "prayer before resorting to medication."[4]

In the preface to *Primitive Physic*, Wesley again made it clear that he preferred "plants and roots" over "chemical, or exotic, or compound medicine." And in his 1775 post-script to *Primitive Physic*, Wesley wrote, "I have once more ventured to recommend to men of plain, unbiased reason such remedies as air, water, milk, whey, honey, treacle, salt, vinegar and common English herbs, with a few foreign medicines, almost equally cheap, safe and common." The practice of compounding medicines, he taught, served "only to swell the apothecary's bill," adding "possibly on purpose, to prolong the distemper that the Dr. and the apothecary may divide the spoil."[5] Elsewhere Wesley decried the popularity of "foul, hard-named exotics" over simple natural remedies, such as cold water and sea water. The fashionability of such remedies was, according to Wesley, "to the utter confusion of common sense."[6]

There was a theological underpinning, of course, for Wesley's preferences. According to theologian Melanie

Dobson Hughes, Wesley "felt that using organic, local ingredients honored God's provisioning for disease through creation—simple medicines paralleled his plain and simple gospel theology—medicine and salvation made accessible for everyone."[7] Randy Maddox suggests, "Wesley may have viewed the modern privileging of chemical medicines over plants as a failure to trust in God's long-standing provisions for dealing with the effects of sin."[8]

We might reasonably infer therefore that Wesley's preference for "organic, local ingredients" in medicines suggests he would have a similar bias toward "organic, local" food that can be grown and prepared by anyone, rather than created in laboratories and factories. He might well believe that God provided such naturally grown food to nourish us and maintain our health in a fallen sinful world.

And what about GMOs? While many believe they are dangerous, the evidence to support their claims is controversial. The current scientific consensus is that GMOs are safe for human consumption. Any Wesleyan objection to GMOs would therefore likely be based on the belief that they are unnatural, rather than unsafe. Biblical scholar Ellen Davis has argued that the widespread use of GMOs may be seen as analogous to the practice of sowing two kinds of seed together, prohibited in Scripture "because it trespasses on the realm of the holy."[9] If Wesley found any such argument persuasive, it might bias him against genetically modified foods. It seems more likely, however, that Wesley would disfavor GMOs on the grounds that using them amounts to a manipulation of God's creation and a rejection of what God has naturally provided to nourish humanity. Wesley might, for example, find merit in the claim of activist and industrial food critic Vandana

Shiva that "GMO" should be understood to stand for "God, move over."[10] And for those adhering to a Wesleyan food ethic by choosing to eat only nutritious foods, the question of the safety of GMO foods will be moot, as GMO ingredients are found almost entirely in processed unhealthy foods, and very rarely in natural whole foods.

2. Wesley's Preference for the Simple over the Complex

As grounds for his objection to chemical-based compound medications, Wesley cited the fact that medicines often contained so many ingredients that "it was scarce possible for common people to know which it was that wrought the cure," as they were composed of an "abundance of exotics, neither the nature or names of which their countrymen understood."[11] In other words, the ingredient lists were simply too complex.

The food movement makes a similar objection to processed foods, which are typically created using a long list of virtually unpronounceable chemical ingredients that no ordinary consumer would recognize. Consider, for example, the ingredients in a popular variety of "Frozen Dairy Dessert" (the description that has replaced "ice cream," now that no cream is actually used in the product). In addition to corn syrup, cottonseed oil, whey, and carob bean gum (which might not strike one as appetizing additions to ice cream), it contains mono and diglycerides, carrageenan (a seaweed extract used as a thickener), tara gum, guar gum, caramel color, lactase enzyme, annatto, and vitamin A palmitate. It is unlikely that typical consumers would have any idea what these things are, even though they are intended to eat them. The product also includes "natural flavor" to give it an intense vanilla taste. The flavor is not derived from vanilla beans, however, but instead is typically extracted from wood pulp or, in some cases, from castoreum, which is produced from the dried and macerated castor sac/anal scent glands of beavers.

The "ice cream" ingredient list is actually modest by comparison to most processed foods. A popular brand of snack cookie, for example, has forty-five ingredients, including corn syrup, folic acid, cottonseed oil, soybean oil, thiamine mononitrate, ammonium bicarbonate, dextrose, polysorbate 60, sorbitan monostearate, soy lecithin, mono and diglycerides, corn starch, caramel color, carrageenan, red dye 40, sorbic acid, and yellow dye 5.[12] A strawberry milkshake from a popular fast-food chain has fifty-nine ingredients, most of which are chemical additives and none of which are strawberries.[13] Consider, by comparison, the ingredient list for an organic tomato purchased at a farmers' market: tomato.

Michael Pollan includes among his "food rules" avoiding any food that has ingredients no normal human being would keep in the pantry, any foods that have more than five ingredients, and any food that has ingredients a typical third grader could not pronounce.[14] Wesley would likely find that to be sensible advice. Given that he objected to medicines composed of complicated mixes of exotic ingredients, there seems to be no reason to think he would favor *foods* that are.

3. Wesley's Environmental Ethic

Another reason the food movement favors organically produced foods is that because they are grown and raised without the use of herbicides, pesticides, nitrate-based fertilizers, growth hormones, and nontherapeutic doses of antibiotics, the production method is less harmful to the environment. To determine whether Wesley would be influenced by the food movement's environmental argument, it is necessary to consider whether he would be inclined toward what we now call environmentalism.

Although "ecology was not on the theological agenda in Wesley's day,"[15] there is within Wesley's work an environmental ethic suggestive of an affinity for what we now call "environmentalism" or "creation care." Wesley affirmed the importance of all of God's creation, writing in the third of his thirteen discourses on the Sermon on the Mount,

> God is in all things, and . . . we are to see the Creator in the glass [eye] of every creature . . . We should use and look upon nothing as separate from God, which indeed is a kind of practical atheism; but, with a true magnificence of thought, survey heaven and earth, and all that is therein, as contained by God in the hollow of his hand, who by his intimate presence holds them all in being, who pervades and actuates the whole created frame, and is, in a true sense, the soul of universe.

In his sermons "The New Creation" and "The General Deliverance," Wesley demonstrated his belief that God's ultimate purpose includes saving *all* of creation, not just humanity, and that humans should model their behavior in anticipation of the final new creation. Pastor and professor Kenneth Loyer concludes, "Given the cosmic dimension of the new creation that Wesley came to emphasize, it may be possible to build on Wesley by applying the same principle—the call for human beings to imitate our merciful God—toward environmental concerns as well."[16]

Environmentalist Wesley?

Was Wesley an environmentalist? Wesley scholar Howard Snyder devotes a chapter of his book *Yes in Christ: Wesleyan Reflections on Gospel, Mission and Culture* to answering that very question. While acknowledging that "environmental concern was not yet on the radar in Wesley's day," Snyder wrote:

> At the level of basic principles, it seems a Wesleyan environmental ethic should be fairly obvious and straightforward. Wesley's accent on love for God and neighbor means loving all that God has made (including the created order) and everything that impinges on human well-being (as the health of the environment surely does). Wesley's insistence on "disinterested love for all" certainly carries creation stewardship implications. His emphases on the image of God and "the wisdom of God in creation" likewise are relevant.[17]

Observing an environmental trajectory in Wesley's thinking, Snyder concludes:

> I suggest four ecological principles that Wesleyans can own and that can contribute significantly to larger discussions about environmental steward-ship . . . First, love of God and neighbor extends to all of creation . . . Second, linked with love is the call to stewardship . . . Third, Wesley's emphasis on "social Christianity" and "social holi-ness" carries creation-care implications. . . . Fourth, Wesley's economic sensitivity has creation-care implications.[18]

Likewise Wesley scholar Randy Maddox argues:

> The suggestions that Wesley had an ecological ethic
> will likely strike readers as anachronistic. Yet . . .
> he stood out in his contemporary Western setting
> as a notable exception in affirming God's ulti-
> mate purpose of restoring all creation. It would
> be reasonable to expect him to have encouraged
> penultimate expressions of this purpose; and indeed
> he did express a concern that was rare in his day for
> humane treatment of animals. It is possible to iden-
> tify the foundations for an ecological ethic drawing
> on such comments. The more important point is
> that Wesley's basic theological perspective is condu-
> cive to an ecological ethic.[19]

Elsewhere Maddox identifies within Wesley's work
a theocentric environmental ethic, in which the ideal
relationship of humanity to creation is one of "modest
stewardship, where we devote our distinctive gifts to
upholding God's intentions for the balance and flourishing of all creation."[20]

Despite the fact that he may never have addressed
the subject directly, given Wesley's love for the natural
order and humanity's place in it, it is easy to conclude
that he would comfortably identify with Christians who
promote environmentalism, rather than those who are
indifferent toward (or contemptuous of) it. In his sermon
"The Good Steward," Wesley affirmed that we are mere
stewards of all we come to possess or control, obligated to
use it as best serves God, its true owner.

> Now, this is exactly the case of every man, with
> relation to God. We are not at liberty to use what
> he has lodged in our hands as *we* please, but as he

pleases, who alone is the possessor of heaven and earth, and the Lord of every creature. We have no right to dispose of anything we have, but according to His will, seeing we are not proprietors of any of these things; they are all, as our Lord speaks, *allotria*, belonging to another person; nor is anything properly our own, in the land of our pilgrimage. We shall not receive *ta idia*, our own things, till we come to our own country. Eternal things only are our own: With all these temporal things we are barely entrusted by another, the Disposer and Lord of all. And he entrusts us with them on this express condition, —that we use them only as our Master's goods, and according to the particular directions which he has given us in his Word.[21]

It seems reasonable therefore that Wesley would easily extend this concept to include our care of the earth, the natural environment, farmland, farm animals, our bodies, and our neighbors.

Thus Theodore Runyon concludes:

Wesley identifies our misuse of the earth, our seeing it apart from its existence in God and apart from God's life in it, as "practical atheism," a sin and offense against the Creator whom we are called to see "in the glass of every creature." Not only humanity images God, therefore, but every creature reflects the love and care of the Creator. And the unity of creation is grasped in the way in which God surrounds and sustains us all. When we deal with the earth and its resources, and when we deal with our fellow creature, we are dealing with God.

For Wesley, therefore, sanctifying faith can in no wise be divorced from care for the environment. To see things truly, to be "pure in heart," is to find ourselves again "in the family of nature," to overcome the ignorance and indifference that have made us "strangers" to that which sustains us, and joyfully to take up the spiritual-physical disciplines and sacrifices necessary not only to protect the earth but to keep covenant with generations yet unborn. For "social holiness" today includes not only our link to all present inhabitants of the planet but to future generations for whom, as stewards, we hold the earth in trust. There can be no holiness today that is not social holiness shaped by this task, and no spirituality not nurtured and emboldened by the *Creator Spirit*.[22]

If, as these scholars suggest, Wesley's views dispose him favorably toward what we now know as environmentalism, then it is reasonable to conclude that he would favor the more environmentally friendly nature of organic agriculture.

Wesley Would Prefer Animals Raised Organically

Wesley's insistence on the humane treatment of animals, and his preference for the natural over the synthetic, would incline him toward organically raised animal products as well. Given his generally unsympathetic view of pharmaceuticals, he might be particularly distressed by the massive amounts of antibiotics administered to animals in nonorganic concentrated animal feeding operations, only in part to protect them from diseases. Leo

Horrigan, Jay Graham, and Shawn McKenzie of Johns Hopkins University's Center for a Livable Future wrote:

> Giving antibiotics to animals in low doses has been found to accelerate growth by making the conversion of feed to weight gain more efficient. As a result, antibiotics are used routinely and on a massive scale in IFAP (Industrial Food Animal Production). In North Carolina alone, the volume of antibiotics used as a feed supplement has been estimated to exceed all U.S. antibiotic use in human medicine.
>
> [Sixty] to 80 percent of antibiotic use in the United States is accounted for by IFAP's use of antibiotics as growth promoters. A relatively small percentage of antibiotic use in IFAP is to treat sick animals, although the exact percentage is unknown because industry is not required to report these data. Much of what is needed for therapeutic purposes is the direct result of the IFAP practice of severely crowding large numbers of food animals into small, unsanitary spaces—thereby increasing the chance that diseases will spread through their populations—and feeding animals an unnatural diet (e.g., raising cattle on grains instead of grass).[23]

This antibiotic overuse has resulted in the emergence of antibiotic-resistant bacteria, giving rise to concerns that strains will develop capable of infecting humans, for which antibiotics will be ineffective. Thus, creating a very dangerous public health risk.

> Numerous studies support a strong link between the introduction of antibiotics into animal feeds and an increased prevalence of drug-resistant organisms isolated from food animals. Those resistant strains

of disease-causing organisms can pose public health threats through food routes and environmental routes.

In the United States and Europe, antibiotic-resistant disease-causing organisms are highly prevalent in meat and poultry products, including organisms that are resistant to the broad-spectrum antibiotics penicillin, tetracycline, and erythromycin. Animals supplied antibiotics in their feed contain a higher prevalence of multidrug-resistant E. coli than animals produced on organic farms without exposure to antibiotics and the same disparity shows up when one compares the foods produced by these two styles of production.[24]

In a 2012 study, *Consumer Reports* magazine tested pork chops and ground pork from supermarkets, finding nearly 70 percent of it to be contaminated with antibiotic-resistant bacteria. The study also discovered traces of the porcine growth hormone ractopamine in 20 percent of the pork sampled.[25]

The National Antimicrobial Resistance Monitoring System (NARMS) of the Center for Disease Control reported similar findings after testing chicken, turkey, and beef:

In 2011, the latest year available, NARMS detected Salmonella in 12 percent of the chicken samples that it tested. About three-quarters of the bugs were resistant to at least one antibiotic, and more than a quarter were resistant to at least five classes of antibiotics. That's eight times the level of multiple resistance found in 2002. Salmonella also turned up in 12 percent of the ground turkey samples. About three-quarters of the bacteria were resistant to at least one antibiotic and 19 percent—double the percentage found in 2002—were resistant to at least five classes of antibiotics.

E. coli was detected in two-thirds of the beef and around 40 percent of the pork samples. Roughly half of the E. coli on pork and a fifth of the E. coli on beef were resistant to at least one antibiotic. About 1 percent of the E. coli on each meat was resistant to at least five classes of antibiotics. For beef, that's triple the percentage found in 2002, and for pork, it's one-third the level.

"The evidence is unequivocal that drug-resistant pathogens have contaminated meat and other animal foods and infected people with drug-resistant infections," says [Lance] Price [an environmental health scientist at George Washington University]. "What we don't know is the full extent of it."[26]

In light of his passionate insistence on a simple diet of nutritious food, it seems reasonable to conclude that Wesley would not approve of eating the meat factory-raised animals contaminated with antibiotic-resistant bacteria. Rather, he would prefer meat from animals raised organically.

"Nothing is small if it touches conscience."

Finally, in assessing where Wesley would come down on the question of organic food, it is important to keep in mind that he would disfavor the use of any food that is harmful to health, even if the harmful effects were not certain or severe. Put differently, Wesley would object to foods that may be injurious to health, even only to a small degree.

Thus, in his "Letter to a Friend Concerning Tea," Wesley responded to the objection that tea is not as harmful as liquor by saying: "I do not believe it is. But it is hurtful. And that is enough. The question does not turn on the degree of hurtfulness." Responding to the further objection that drinking tea, even if harmful, was only a "small thing," Wesley wrote, "Nay, nothing is small if it touches conscience. Much less is it a small thing to preserve my own or my brother's health."

For Wesley, anything that "tends to impair health" is plainly forbidden, while "every probable means of preserving or restoring" health must be used. If Wesley accepted the idea that organic food is a probable means of preserving or restoring health, then he would endorse it, even over an objection that an organic diet is a small thing compared to other means of preserving or restoring health. Likewise, if the argument that organic food production is less damaging to the environment and to farm animals should touch Wesley's conscience, then he would favor it and consider it no small thing.

Given Wesley's bias in favor of things and practices that are simple and "natural," given that there is evidence that organic food is more nutritious than conventional food, and given the arguments that organic production is less harmful to farm animals and to the environment, it seems likely therefore that Wesley would prefer food raised organically to that which is not. It seems reasonable to conclude, therefore, that just as he would join the food movement in insisting on nutritious whole-food diets, and in opposing the consumption of milk, eggs and meat from animals raised in CAFOs, Wesley would also join with the food movement in urging a diet of primarily organically-produced food.

For Discussion

1. Do you choose organic food for your family? Why or why not? What do you consider when making that decision? Are any of the considerations theological?

2. Can you think of any reasons why Wesley might prefer organic food, other than those mentioned in this chapter? Can you think of any reasons he might not prefer organic food?

3. How do you think Wesley would feel about the modern environmentalist movement? Where might he agree with it, and what areas of conflict might exist?

4. Is there anything in this chapter that surprised you or was new to you? What are your thoughts about the organic versus conventional food debate?

5. Have any of the subjects mentioned in this chapter ever been discussed in any sermon or Bible study at your church? If so, how was it received? If not, why do think that is the case?

7

Globalization and Local Economies

What we must do is simple: we must shorten the distance that our food is transported so that we are eating more and more from local supplies, more and more to the benefit of local farmers, and more and more to the satisfaction of local consumers . . . We should not be discouraged to find that local food economies can grow only gradually; it is better that they should grow gradually. But as they grow they will bring about a significant return of power, wealth and health to the people.

—WENDELL BERRY
"Farming and the Global Economy," 1995

We have lately extended the British Empire almost over the globe. We have carried our laurels into Africa, into Asia, into the burning and the frozen climes of America. And what have we brought thence? All the elegance of vice which either the eastern or western world could afford.

—JOHN WESLEY
"National Sins and Miseries," 1775

THE GLOBALIZATION OF the modern industrial food system would be astonishing to Wesley. In a typical grocery store these days, one can find nearly any item of produce imaginable, at any time of year—grapes from Chile, honey from Argentina, garlic from China, orange juice from Brazil . . . the list goes on and on. Indeed, it is likely that the food in your last meal came from at least five states away from you (and perhaps much farther than that). Consider the case of the popular chocolate/hazelnut spread Nutella:

> Some 250,000 tons of Nutella are now sold across 75 countries around the world every year, according to the OECD. But that's not what's amazing about it. Nutella, it turns out, is a perfect example of what globalization has meant for popular foodstuffs: Not only is it sold everywhere, but its ingredients are sourced from all over the place too.
>
> Even though Ferrero International, which makes the stuff, is headquartered in Italy, it has factories in Europe, Russia, North America and South America. And while certain inputs are supplied locally—like, say, the plastic for the bottles or milk—many others are shipped from all over the world. The hazelnuts are from Turkey; the palm oil is from Malaysia; the cocoa is from Nigeria; the sugar is from either Brazil or Europe; and the vanilla flavoring is from France.[1]

Here's another example: a steer from a farm in Virginia might be sold at a livestock auction, then transported to a feedlot in Kansas, where it will it be fattened on corn grown in Iowa, before being trucked to a slaughterhouse in Texas. There its meat will be ground and aggregated with that of thousands of other steers from all over the country, then shipped to a facility in California, where it will be processed into frozen patties, and then trucked across the country to be sold at fast-food restaurants. A cheeseburger sold at a McDonald's in Kentucky, then, might contain a bit of the Virginia steer, on a bun made in part from wheat grown in Minnesota, along with lettuce from California, tomatoes from Mexico, cheese from cows milked in Wisconsin, pickles from cucumbers grown in Florida, flavorings manufactured in New Jersey, and spices and additives from literally all over the world. The seventy-three ingredients in a McDonald's Big Mac, for example, include chemical additives, such as ammonium chloride, sodium stearoyl lactylate, sodium phosphate, polysorbate 80, and azodicarbonamide, that did not originate on any farm.[2] In fact, the vast majority of the food additives and vitamin fortifications found in food these days are produced synthetically, in China.[3]

Howard Snyder and Joel Scandrette, in their book *Salvation Means Creation Healed*, tell us:

> Every person should be able to answer the four most basic food questions: What is it? Where did it come from? How did it get here? Is it good for me? But most Americans today and millions of other people in the increasingly globalized food market simply cannot answer these most basic questions. If they look at the list of ingredients, they are quickly mystified by unknown chemical compounds and unfamiliar technical terms. We simply have no idea how much of our food comes from factory farms, laboratories, and fossil fuels, rather from healthy farms that nurture and preserve the earth. Often we simply do not know what we are eating.[4]

The Local Food Movement and Seasonal Eating

There is a strong bias within the food movement in favor of locally grown food and community-based food economies. Indeed, the movement is sometimes called the *local* food movement. This preference for locally grown food derives from, among other factors, a belief that food grown locally tends to be fresher, and therefore better tasting. Farmers producing food intended for direct sale to local consumers need not be so concerned with shelf life. Further, whereas industrial produce is often picked before it is ripe—sometimes weeks before it finally reaches the consumer—locally grown food can be allowed to ripen naturally on the vine. Since produce begins to lose nutritional value once it is picked those fruits and vegetables grown and sold nearby are more nutrient-dense. Also, whereas industrial farm products must have the uniformity of appearance demanded by supermarkets and restaurants, farms selling to local consumers are not troubled with how their products will look or keep on a grocery store shelf. Thus on local farms, and at the local markets they serve, it is often possible to find traditional heirloom varieties of produce that are unavailable in supermarkets.

There is also within the food movement a partiality toward seasonal eating, meaning a diet emphasizing produce that is in season in one's community at the time it is eaten, which many believe to be a more natural diet, having attendant health benefits. Not only that, but purchasing locally grown food fosters and supports resilient local economies. Community-based economies are considered less damaging to the environment and more sustainable than the globalized industrial food system. For so-called locavores it is important to be able to identify the food with the farmers who grew it. They want to be able to shake the hands that feed them, knowing that the person who picked their food loves the land it grew on—neither of which is possible in the faceless industrial food system.

Would Wesley Be a Locavore?

So, would Wesley join with the food movement in advocating community-based food economies? While he never specifically addressed the issue, it is possible to locate within his writings and teachings evidence suggestive of a preference for community-based food systems.

As with all of his thinking on matters involving food and human health, we can expect that Wesley's views would be informed principally by the Bible, and secondarily by his mentor Dr. George Cheyne. In the absence of any biblical authority to the contrary, Wesley could be expected to follow Cheyne's lead.

Cheyne advocated a diet of simple, locally grown food, arguing that the food and natural remedies that God had made available in a particular community are those that are best suited for the health of the people living in that community. In his book *The English Malady* (1733), he wrote:

> It is highly probable that the infinitely wise Author of our nature has provided proper remedies and reliefs in every climate for all the distempers and diseases incident to their respective inhabitants, if in his Providence he has necessarily placed them there: and certainly the food and physic proper and peculiar to the middling sort of each country and climate is the best of any possible for the support of the creatures he has unavoidably placed there, provided only that they follow the simplicity of nature, the dictates of reason and experience, do not lust after foreign delicacies: as we see by the health and cheerfulness of the middling sort of almost all nations. . . .

In medicines as in food (medicines being only a
more rare and less natural kind of food), that which
is common to the middling sort of every country,
and which has the approbation of the generality of
its inhabitants and is suited to the constitution of the
community, is generally the most beneficial, since it
is the experience and observation of the generality
that makes them common: and special or particular
things, or rarities, are justly to be suspected.[5]

Cheyne specifically argued that food imported from
far away is less nutritious, presumably because it originated in other climates and environments, rather than in
those local to the persons eating the food.

But where the luxury and diseases of all the nations of
the globe are brought together, mingled and blended,
and perhaps heightened by the difference of climates,
there is an absolute necessity that the materials of
physic, and the methods of cure, should be varied and
extended in equal proportion: which is the cause of
the multiplicity of our medicines, and the necessity
that physicians are under to know almost everything
that is noble in nature, for the use of physic: and to
bring from each country and climate the proper anti-
dote for the distempers brought from thence.[6]

While contemporary nutrition experts might not
agree with all of Cheyne's reasoning, they would likely
concur with his conclusion. In a report published by the
USDA's Economic Research Service in 2010, a team
of researchers concluded, "Produce that is allowed to
ripen fully on the vine—as is usually the case for local
and seasonal fruits and vegetables—has higher levels of

nutrients than produce ripened artificially in warehouses. Additionally, nutrient levels start to decrease after harvest, so a shorter distance from field to plate is best."[7]

As with so many other things, Wesley would likely accept and adopt Cheyne's conclusions. It seems especially likely given that Cheyne's preference for locally-grown food was rooted in theological and nutritional considerations that Wesley consistently followed in all other respects. We can expect, therefore, that Wesley would join with Cheyne, and also with the contemporary food movement, in urging a diet of simple locally-produced foods. There are other indications in Wesley's writings of a preference for community-based economies as well. What we now know as "globalization" was in its infancy during Wesley's day, existing in the form of a colonial system whereby empires such as Great Britain extracted the wealth of less-developed societies. Wesley saw that one effect of this commerce was increased gluttony:

> And are we not a generation of epicures? Is not our belly our god? Are not eating and drinking our chief delight, our highest happiness? Is it not the main study (I fear, the only study) of many honourable men to enlarge the pleasure of tasting? When was luxury (not in food only, but in dress, furniture, equipage) carried to such a height in Great Britain ever since it was a nation? We have lately extended the British Empire almost over the globe. We have carried our laurels into Africa, into Asia, into the burning and the frozen climes of America. And what have we brought thence? All the elegance of vice which either the eastern or western world could afford.[8]

Certainly this sentiment does not seem favorable to a globalized economy.

Wesley also saw danger in the consolidation of farms into fewer owners. In his day the danger was that the gentlemen who acquired the farmland would not use it for the production of food, thereby leading to a scarcity of food and higher prices. Wesley described the consequences in his essay "Thoughts on the Present Scarcity of Provisions."

> The land which was some years ago divided between ten or twenty little farmers, and enabled them comfortably to provide for their families, is now generally engrossed by one great farmer. One farms an estate of a thousand a year, which formerly maintained ten or twenty. Every one of these little farmers kept a few swine, with some quantity of poultry; and, having little money, was glad to send his bacon, or pork, or fowls and eggs to market continually. Hence the markets were plentifully served; and plenty created cheapness. But at present, the great, the gentlemen-farmers are above attending to these little things. They breed no poultry or swine, unless for their own use; consequently they send none to market. Hence it is not strange if two or three of these, living near a market town, occasion such a scarcity of these things, by preventing the former supply, that the price of them is double or treble to what it was before.[9]

In the essay, Wesley examined the reasons for escalating food prices, which were creating hardships for the poor. He attributed the problem in part to the luxurious diets, wastefulness, and overconsumption of the wealthy, but also in part to a local food system that was not meeting the needs of its community. Charles Wallace and Jeremy Gregory summarize Wesley's concerns:

> [For Wesley] the evils that caused the starvation of many were several. Distilling soaked up too much corn. The brisk market in horses (for all the carriages in Britain as well as for export to France) brought on an equine population explosion, which overwhelmed the market for oats, and as more people ventured into horse breeding, fewer cattle and sheep were raised. What we might refer to as eighteenth-century agribusiness, the buying up of small holdings by gentlemen farmers, meant that fewer people were supplying local markets with pork, poultry and eggs.[10]

Wesley thus recognized the benefit of productive diversified local farms and the risks accompanying their absence.

It is possible to see within Wesley's argument a preference for local food-based, diversified agriculture based on family farms, and a corresponding natural opposition to consolidated, large-scale industrial agriculture under the control of multinational corporations. Although he was addressing a different concern, it seems clear he had a degree of sympathy for the little farmers and the benefits they bring to a community. It is easy to imagine, therefore, that he would prefer the community and relationship-building that comes from supporting local farmers, rather than patronizing faceless and amoral industrial agricultural corporations by shopping at supermarkets and grocery stores.

The Social Justice Implications of Globalization of Food

Advocates of community-based economies and local food systems note the environmental damage associated with the industrialized system and its reliance on fossil fuels to transport food such great distances, when it is arguably unnecessary to do so. The massive monocultural operations used to produce food in the industrial model are also harmful to the environment. Further, the industrial food model characteristically relies on low-paid and sometimes exploited farm labor, typically temporary migrant workers from poor, less-developed places, such as rural Mexico. None of these factors would be lost on Wesley. As with all other matters of concern to him, he would take into account the bigger picture of social justice.

In his sermon "The Use of Money," Wesley tempered his famous advice to "gain all you can," with the proviso that a Christian may not "gain by hurting a neighbor in his body. Therefore we may not sell anything that tends to impair health." Thus, he attacked those who profit from selling liquor, calling them "poisoners" and saying "the curse of God" is upon them. But Wesley didn't limit his critique to sellers of liquor, instead aiming it broadly at anyone profiting from damaging the health of others. In the sermon he specifically named "those who have anything to do with . . . victualling houses" (restaurants) as potentially "ministering . . . either directly or indirectly . . . to intemperance." This, he declared, "certainly none can do who has any fear of God, or any real desire for pleasing Him."[11] Wesley would therefore object to Christians owning (as well as patronizing) fast-food restaurants, grocery stores, and convenience stores selling food that is damaging to others' health.

Directed away from merchants selling health-impairing food, Wesley's followers might naturally be expected to gravitate toward farmers' markets and the local food movement instead.

Being something of an ascetic, Wesley would not likely concern himself much with the taste advantages of local food. He would insist, however, that food be ethically sourced, and it seems likely that he would favor a food economy revolving around tens of thousands of small, diversified farms, tended by industrious and ethical families, over an industrialized food system largely under the control of a few amoral multinational corporations. Given Wesley's deep concern over diet, and his strong feelings on animal welfare, it is also likely he would prefer a food system in which the consumer can know farmers personally, and have some comfort level as to whether the farmers' practices are safe, ethical, and humane. And of course, Wesley's insistence on a nutritious diet would incline him toward locally produced food.

So would Wesley be a "locavore" if he lived in our contemporary society? The answer would seem to be a clear yes.

For Discussion

1. Think of the last meal you ate. Do you know where the food came from? Who grew and picked the food? Does that matter to you? Why or why not?

2. Can you think of any good reasons to prefer food produced locally? Do any of those reasons directly relate to Christian faith?

3. Is the food you ate in your last meal available from local sources? Does it grow in your climate? Does it grow at this time of year? What are the consequences of relying on diets of food imported from great distances away?

4. Leaving aside any moral, ethical, or religious concerns, are there any purely practical advantages to favoring locally grown food? Are there any disadvantages?

5. Are there farmers in your congregation or community? If not, why not? If so, have you ever eaten food raised on their farms?

8

Wesley in Conflict with the Food Movement

We are now pretty clearly involved in a crisis of health, one of the wonders of which is its immense profitability both to those who cause it and to those who propose to cure it.

—WENDELL BERRY
"Health Is Membership," 1994

Is there a character more despicable than even that of a liar? Perhaps there is; even that of an epicure. And are we not a generation of epicures? Is not our belly our god? Are not eating and drinking our chief delight, our highest happiness? Is it not the main study (I fear, the only study) of many honourable men to enlarge the pleasure of tasting?

—JOHN WESLEY
"National Sins and Miseries," 1775

THE PRINCIPAL THEMES of the food movement are consonant with Wesley's work and ethics. Wesley shared the food movement's passion for healthy, nutritious diets, as well as its emphasis on the humane and ethical treatment of animals. Wesley's ethics and teachings likewise seem supportive of the food movement's preference for food that is organically and naturally produced, and for local community–based food systems. If John Wesley were alive today, there is very good reason to believe he would be an ally of the food movement and would join it in opposition to the prevailing industrial food system.

That is not to say, however, that Wesley would find no fault with the contemporary food movement. What objections might he have to the food movement? What criticisms might he level at it? Are there things about the movement with which Wesley would not agree? To what degree is it *inconsistent* with his ethics and theology?

Certainly there are things about our culture's focus on food with which Wesley might find fault. Let us examine his possible criticisms.

Is the Food Movement Too Secular?

Wesley would likely find fault with the predominantly secular nature of the food movement. Wesley was, after all, first and foremost a Christian evangelist. His strong opinions on nutritious food, the sinfulness of over-consumption, the humane treatment of animals, and benevolent, sustainable economies were all grounded in his religious beliefs and in his understanding of God and Scripture. To the extent that the food movement exists independently of any underlying religious rationale for such things, Wesley would insist that it lacks proper focus. For Wesley, eating locally grown, nourishing, organic food, in moderation, while avoiding consuming the meat, eggs, and milk from animals raised in cruel and unnat-ural conditions would be good and commendable things. But if these things were done without giving credit to God, and not as part of an overall life characterized by a striving for Christian holiness, integrity, and simplicity, Wesley would believe them to be spiritually incomplete and ultimately unsatisfying.

That does not mean, however, that there would be no place in the food movement for John Wesley. In fact, there is a robust and vibrant Christian element to the movement, within which Wesley would fit comfortably.

Christians who are engaged with the movement tend to be motivated at least in part by a desire to better serve and honor the Creator, and to reflect that desire in their food choices. Further, Christian communities are often not satisfied merely with improving their own health and diets, instead often seeking ways to help deliver natural and nutritious food to the poor and underprivileged as well, such as by promoting the development of community and church gardens. Likewise many Christians are advocates of the food movement as part of a broader appeal for simpler and more sustainable lifestyles. Indeed, many Christians are attracted to the contemporary food movement for the very reasons that Wesley would be.

This explicitly Christian subset of the movement resonates powerfully with the teachings of Wesley, and it is there that he would be most at home. Respect for God's creation, concern for the poor, living simply and unpretentiously—these are recurring themes in Wesley's teachings just as they are in the Christian element of the food movement. If John Wesley were alive today, he would be a natural leader in that segment of the movement.

Is the Food Movement Elitist?

Another potential objection would derive from the allegations of food-based elitism that have been frequently directed at today's food movement. Wesley would certainly object to status consumption of any sort, including purchases of food designed to impress others or advance social status. Wesley frequently criticized the extravagance and waste associated with food delicacies, and he would no doubt join in criticism of the food movement where he recognized conspicuous consumption and mere trendiness. Wesley declared, "The love of God is not in me . . . if I am a lover of honour or praise, of dress, or of good eating and drinking,"[1]

But as food-writer Tanya Denckla Cobb correctly says of the charge of elitism, "Those who brand the local food movement as elitist are more myopic than wrong, as elitists can be found in any movement."[2] Any tendency of the food movement toward cultural elitism or status-seeking consumption would certainly draw Wesley's fire, but given his deep-rooted theological commitment to the principles that the food movement promotes, we could expect that if this is a fault of the movement he would challenge the fault (and seek to overcome it), rather than reject the movement itself.

Is the Food Movement Too Focused on Self-Pleasure?

Likewise, Wesley might be expected to be critical of the food movement's emphasis on the pleasures of eating well. Given his stinging indictment of "epicures,"[3] Wesley might not be expected to be sympathetic to a movement focused on increasing one's personal pleasure in food. Yet he would find no fault in enjoying the pleasures that come from simple, wholesome diets, and likewise the food movement's attention to the pleasures of eating good food, understood in its context, would not likely trouble him.

The emphasis on pleasure is probably most evident in the Slow Food movement, which originated in Italy in the mid-1980s and combines concerns with environmentalism, fair trade, and justice for food producers with an emphasis on enjoying the pleasures of preparing and eating good food.[4] Carlo Petrini, the founder of the Slow Food movement, describes himself as a "gastronome." A close examination of how Petrini defines the word, however, suggests that there is, in fact, significant room for consonance with Wesley's concerns for social justice: "I am a gastronome. No, not the glutton with no sense of restraint whose enjoyment of food is greater the more plentiful and forbidden it is. No, not a fool who is given to the pleasures of the table and indifferent to how the food got there. I like to imagine the hands of the people who grew it, transported it, processed it, and cooked it before it was served to me."[5]

Further, while it is true that Wesley could be critical of eating solely for the sake of pleasure, it is unlikely that he would have any objection to taking pleasure in one's food, provided it is nutritious and ethically sourced, and so long as the poor are not being deprived of it in order to gratify the pleasures of the rich.

Wesley clearly connected his objection to the pleasure-seeking love of food with his concern for the poor in his sermon "On God's Vineyard":

O ye that have riches in possession, once more hear the word of the Lord! Ye that are rich in this world, that have food to eat, and raiment to put on, and something over, are you clear of the curse of loving the world? Are you sensible of your danger? Do you feel, "How hardly will they that have riches enter into the kingdom of heaven?" Do you continue unburned in the midst of the fire? Are you untouched with the love of the world? Are you clear from the desire of the flesh, the desire of the eyes, and the pride of life? Do you "put a knife to your throat," when you sit down to meat, lest your table should be a snare to you? Is not your belly your god? Is not eating and drinking, or any other pleasure of sense, the greatest pleasure you enjoy? Do not you seek happiness in dress, furniture, pictures, gardens, or anything else that pleases the eye? Do not you grow soft and delicate; unable to bear cold, heat, the wind or the rain, as you did when you were poor? Are you not increasing in goods, laying up treasures on earth; instead of restoring to God in the poor, not so much, or so much, but all that you can spare? Surely, "it is easier for a camel to go through the eye of a needle, than for a rich man to enter into the kingdom of heaven!"[6]

For Wesley, in determining whether taking pleasure in food is objectionable, it is important to assess whether that pleasure comes at the expense of the poor.

Moreover, while Wesley would be critical of pleasure-seeking for its own sake, he would not necessarily object to enjoying wholesome food. Indeed, as Wallace and Gregory note, "His critique of luxuriousness to one side, Wesley seems to have enjoyed his food and expected others to do the same."[7] Cheerfulness, Wesley wrote, "is highly proper at a Christian meal," adding that "agreeable food" should be "seasoned" with thankfulness. In fact, Wesley specifically rejected the notion that Christians must necessarily deny themselves food that is pleasing, concluding instead that a person with a "pure heart" may prefer pleasing food to "unpleasing, though equally wholesome, food, as a means of increasing thankfulness, with a single eye to God, who giveth us all things richly to enjoy: On the same principle, he may smell to a flower, or eat a bunch of grapes, or take any other pleasure which does not lessen but increase his delight in God."[8] On another occasion Wesley wrote, "It is not possible to avoid all pleasure, even of sense, without destroying the body. Neither doth God require it at our hands; it is not his will concerning us."[9] Neglecting the poor while treating one's belly as a god would clearly be offensive to Wesley. Cheerfully and thankfully taking pleasure in simple, nutritious, and ethically sourced meals, however, would not.

Likewise Wesley would likely be sympathetic to the Slow Food movement's opposition to fast food and the loss of the simple pleasures derived from preparing and eating good food. Slow Food historian Geoff Andrews notes that "Slow Food's critique of fast food cannot therefore be separated from a broader critique of Fast Life, in which food becomes the key factor in a broader critique of fast living, with costs as diverse as poor safety and hygiene, obesity, poverty and famine, environmental degradation and global inequality."[10] Closely connected to the Slow Food movement's call for pleasurable eating, therefore, is a deep ethical concern for the social and environmental costs of industrial food, which would resonate with Wesley.

So while Wesley might distance himself from any call for good food that is rooted solely in a desire for pleasure, it seems he would otherwise be sympathetic to the idea of Slow Food. In any event, even if Wesley rejected the Slow Food movement entirely, it is merely a subset of the much larger food movement, within which Wesley would continue to comfortably fit.

Is Local and Organic Food Too Expensive?

The criticism that local and organic food is more expensive, is unavailable to the poor, and is therefore a privilege only of the affluent, would certainly attract Wesley's careful attention. Wesley frequently urged a simple diet of plain food. He often spoke out against the wasting of money on delicate foods. In his sermon "The Use of Money," Wesley taught specifically that money should not be wasted "in gratifying the desires of the flesh . . . particularly in enlarging the pleasures of tasting." He called for Christians to "despise delicacy and variety, and be content with what plain nature requires."

But, importantly, even as Wesley consistently condemned wasting money on luxuries, he never compromised on his insistence on a healthy diet, and he never suggested that there was anything wrong with spending the money necessary to assure such a diet. "If you desire to be a faithful and a wise steward," Wesley wrote, ". . . first, provide things needful to yourself; food to eat, raiment to put on, whatever nature moderately requires for preserving the body in health and strength." His famous advice to "save all you can," was limited in an important way: "by cutting off every expense which serves *only to indulge foolish desire*" (emphasis added). Wesley would never characterize nutritious food as a foolish desire.

Moreover, in considering how Wesley would respond to the complaint that naturally produced food is too expensive, it is necessary to examine *why* he called for a simple diet. The primary reasons Wesley insisted on plain and inexpensive food were his belief that expensive, fanciful foods were injurious to health and his desire that the money spent on those foods be used instead to help the poor (rather than to destroy one's health). Importantly, however, Wesley never contended that Christians should eat badly in order to save money to give to the poor. Rather, his argument was always twofold: not only was the purchase of expensive food diverting resources from the poor, but it was also less wholesome than simpler food.

Wesley's relationship with tea-drinking well illustrates his ethic. In his 1748 "Letter to a Friend, Concerning Tea" Wesley argued that people should abstain from drinking tea, using the money they would have otherwise spent on tea to benefit the poor. Like most Englishmen of his day, Wesley loved tea. Once he became convinced that tea was bad for his health, however, he gave it up, drinking none for more than twelve years. But in giving up something he deemed harmful to the body, he also recognized that he could simultaneously benefit the poor with the money he would otherwise have spent on it. Thus, in his "Letter to a Friend" Wesley repeatedly emphasized how the money being spent on tea could be used instead to feed the hungry and clothe the naked. Discussing his own savings from having given up tea, he wrote, "I have been enabled hereby to assist in one year above 50 poor with food or raiment, whom I must otherwise have left (for I had begged for them all I could) as hungry and naked as I found them."

But in 1760 Wesley's physician advised him to resume drinking tea for health reasons. Based on this advice, Wesley abandoned his twelve-year abstinence from tea and resumed drinking it frequently. Samuel Rogol, who has studied Wesley's use of tea, has written:

> Certainly, in 1748, Wesley could list abstinence from strong tea as among *his* personal sacrifices on behalf of the evangelical revival. However, once Dr.

Fothergill suggested resumption of the beverage as a benefit to Wesley's health, all of the arguments and suggestions set forth in the "Letter to a Friend" retreated to the darkness of history. From 1758 until the final days of his long life, the Methodist patriarch held fast to his tea cup. Indeed, each of the final ten diary entries—Monday, February 14, 1791, through Wednesday, February 23, 1791— contains at least one reference to Wesley having taken tea. From Thursday, February 17, 1791 through Wednesday, March 2, 1791 (the day of Wesley's death), Elizabeth Ritchie, who nursed him during his final days, maintained a narrative of events; on Sunday morning, February 26—but four days before he died—"with a little of Mr. [Joseph] Bradford's help, Mr. Wesley got up, took a cup of tea, and seemed much better."[11]

Thus, once Wesley became persuaded that tea was in fact beneficial to his health, he resumed drinking it even though it cost him money that he would otherwise have given to the poor. He concluded that spending a little extra money on tea, in order to preserve his health, was more important than refraining from tea (to the detriment of his health) in order to have more money to give to the poor. The importance of this should not be overlooked. Few of the well-known leaders in Christian history have been more insistent upon giving to the poor and living a simple life than John Wesley. Throughout the duration of his ministry, Wesley repeat- edly railed against luxuries, unnecessary spending, and neglect of the poor. "If you have any desire to escape the damnation of hell, give all you can; otherwise I can have no more hope of your salvation than of that of Judas Iscariot," he declared in his sermon "Causes of the Inefficacy of Christianity." Both notoriously frugal and exceedingly generous, Wesley gave away more than £30,000 during his life, "an amount that could have kept a gentleman for a decade,"[12] and he died nearly penniless, believing it would be a sin to do otherwise. "If I leave behind me ten pounds," Wesley wrote, "you and all mankind bear witness against me, that I lived and died a thief and a robber."[13]

Notwithstanding the importance Wesley placed upon giving to the poor and upon living an austere life, however, he never advocated eating cheap, unhealthy food in order to save money, no matter what would be done with the savings. While Wesley contended that it would be sinful for a Christian to possess anything above the plain necessaries and conveniences of life, he considered nutritious food to be necessary. A faithful steward, Wesley argued, first provides his own household with the "things needful for life and godliness," and then uses what remains to care for the poor.[14] Only after providing themselves and their families with "whatever nature moderately requires for preserving the body in health and strength," should persons give their money to the poor.[15] Discussing Jesus' statement that one should not "lay up for yourselves treasures on earth," Wesley wrote, "Neither . . . does he here forbid the providing for ourselves such things as are needful for the body; a sufficiency of plain, wholesome food to eat, and clean raiment to put on. Yea, it is our duty, so far as God puts it into our power, to provide these things also; to the end we may 'eat our own bread,' and be burdensome to no man."[16] Indeed, Wesley was consistently insistent that "we ought not to gain money at the expense of life, nor (which is in effect the same thing) at the expense of our health. You 'render unto God the things that are God's," he concluded, "not only by what you give to the poor, but by what you expend in providing things needful to yourself and your household." Likewise Wesley condemned religious practices that damage one's health. "We may not offer God murder for sacrifice," he wrote, "or destroy our bodies to help our souls."[17]

Thus Wesley considered it a Christian duty to give generously to the poor, but not before spending what was necessary to assure the health of one's own household. For him, knowingly consuming food that is harmful to the body is a sin. Money spent on wholesome food, on the other hand, is money well spent.

Moreover, Wesley would surely consider and take into account how our society is spending the money that it is "saving" by buying less expensive (and less wholesome) food. The reality, of course, is that very few of us are choosing to buy cheap food so we will have more money to give to the poor. Our society spends less of its income on food than any society in history. In Wesley's day the price of food "consumed nearly everything the poor could earn."[18] Today in the United States, on the other hand, less than 10 percent of Americans' disposable income is spent on food, down from approximately 17 percent in 1985, nearly 30 percent in 1950, and more than 40 percent in 1900.[19] By comparison, Europeans today spend about 25 percent of their income on food.[20] For the vast majority of the people in our society, an increase in the amount spent on food simply would not crowd out the other necessities of life. In fact, the additional cost of eating a healthy diet has been estimated to be, on average, only $1.49 per day.[21] Because of the emphasis he placed on the importance of good food and healthy eating, we can expect Wesley would urge people to carefully examine how they are spending their money on items *other* than food, before concluding that they can only afford cheap, health-impairing food.

Of course, for those with very low incomes and those suffering from other forms of food insecurity, only the cheapest food may be available or affordable. Each month, nearly 15 percent of American households experience food insecurity, the threat of having insufficient food.[22] Wesley, who was passionate about seeking to make food more affordable to the poor, would deplore such injustice and challenge a society that permits it to occur. His answer, however, would not be to provide cheap, unhealthy food to the poor, but rather to see that *nutritious* food is made available to those who cannot afford or access it. He would insist (as he did frequently during his lifetime) that Christians stop spending money on frivolous items as long as the poor are unable to afford or access healthy food. Wesley would not, however, argue that Christians should eat unhealthy diets as a way of acquiring money for charitable giving. He would almost certainly consider any such notion to be ridiculous.

It is also important to consider *why* unhealthy food appears to be cheap. As a sophisticated observer of social injustice, Wesley might well be expected to understand that there are hidden costs and externalities associated with industrial food. As theologian Norman Wirzba has written:

> All of our cheap food, however, comes at a very high cost. The sticker price at the store does not reflect the costs associated with eroded and chemically laden soils, poisoned and depleted waters, the burning of vast quantities of fossil fuels, abused animals, abused farm workers, poorly treated and

poorly compensated food-service providers, and the myriad number of diet-related diseases that are causing health-care costs to skyrocket. Our demand for cheap food is slowly degrading and destroying all life on our planet. It is a demand made by a generation of people that is spending the smallest percentage of income on food we have ever known.[23]

Wesley simply would not favor consumption of food produced unethically, however cheap it might be.

Further, the cheapest foods are often sugary, salty, fatty processed foods that are destructive to health and lacking in nutrition. The manufacturers of these foods design their products to create a form of addiction to them, and to profit from the resulting overconsumption. In a *New York Times Magazine* article published in February 2013, in advance of the publication of his book *Salt Sugar Fat: How the Food Giants Hooked Us*, investigative journalist Michael Moss wrote:

The public and the food companies have known for decades now . . . that sugary, salty, fatty foods are not good for us in the quantities that we consume them. So why are the diabetes and obesity and hypertension numbers still spiraling out of control? It's not just a matter of poor willpower on the part of the consumer and a give-the-people-what-they-want attitude on the part of the food manufacturers. What I found, over four years of research and reporting, was a conscious effort—taking place in labs and marketing meetings and grocery-store aisles—to get people hooked on foods that are convenient and inexpensive . . . The biggest hits— be they Coca-Cola or Doritos—owe their success to complex formulas that pique the taste buds enough to be alluring but don't have a distinct, overriding single flavor that tells the brain to stop eating.[24]

Leaving aside the hidden costs of cheap food, the idea that healthy foods are more inherently expensive is itself debatable. In *Sugar Salt Fat* Michael Moss references the work of USDA economists in 2012 who

> sought to refute the perception that healthy foods were more expensive. They acknowledged that this is certainly true when foods are measured by their energy value. Calorie for calorie, broccoli is far more expensive than cookies. But noting that too many calories is, in fact, central to the obesity crisis, the economists developed an alternative calculation. They compared foods by how much they weighed, and by this metric, broccoli had a lower cost, per pound, than cereal and other packaged foods that rely on the high calorie/lightweight pillars of processed food: sugar and fat.[25]

Likewise, as Melanie Warner notes in her book *Pandora's Lunchbox*:

> Although fast food and other processed options are often portrayed as affordable, the reality is that doing your own cooking is almost always cheaper, not to mention more nutritious and satisfying. You can see this cost differential in the frozen food aisles, where processed chicken is anywhere from 30 percent to 100 percent more expensive on a per-ounce basis than the raw stuff over in the meat department. Eating well is in no way a luxury of the rich. We certainly can't all eat at fancy restaurants, but affordable nutritious food is more

available today than it's ever been. Eggs, fresh meat, real cheese, plain yogurt, wholesome grains, half a dozen different kinds of beans and nuts, dozens of different fruits and vegetables—they're all available pretty much any time we want them. The modern supermarket shimmers with a perplexing array of complex pseudo-foods, but it also holds the keys to the most nutritious and varied diet Americans have ever had access to.[26]

Wesley might be expected to understand that the higher cost of wholesome, nutritious foods would not alone make them luxuries or delicacies. Further, if he determined that the money saved by those buying cheaper, less healthy food was then spent on frivolous items or things that diminished health rather than improved it, Wesley likely would conclude that natural food is affordable and that any extra cost is money well spent. Wesley simply would never subordinate nutrition and the preservation of health to frugality or saving money.

Wesley Would Seek to Reform the Movement, Not Reject It

We might expect Wesley to join with those who criticize the elitism of the food movement and its attraction to trend-followers for whom organic food is merely another status symbol. Likewise, we can be sure he would insist on more determined efforts to extend the benefits of natural food to the poor, and not to limit them only to the affluent and well-educated. Wesley's austerity and insistence on temperance would seem to predispose him against any emphasis on the pleasure of good eating (pleasure, as such, being something he never advocated for its own sake), but would not cause him to prefer unpleasing food over tasty food. And of course Wesley would insist that God and personal holiness be central to any food ethic.

Because the food movement is consonant with Wesley's values notwithstanding these possible objections, however, we should expect him to seek to reform or redirect it, even as he embraced it. Whatever criticisms he might have of its manifestations, as an advocate of nutritious, ethically sourced food, Wesley would almost certainly prefer the food movement to the industrial food system.

For Discussion

1. Are you persuaded that Wesley's values naturally align him with the food movement? Why or why not?

2. Is local, organically produced food more expensive than conventional industrial food where you live? How important is price in your determination of what food your family should eat? Is good food unaffordable in your community? Why do you think there is a price difference?

3. Have you seen any evidence of food snobbery, elitism, or judgmentalism about food in your community? Do you ever see it among Christians? If so, why do you think that happens and what is the best way to address it?

4. Based on what you have read so far, do you intend to make any changes to the way you eat or shop for food? Why or why not?

9

Recovering a Wesleyan
Food Ethic

I present to serious and candid men my last and
maturest thoughts, agreeable I hope to Scripture,
reason and Christian antiquity.

—JOHN WESLEY
Preface to *Collected Works*, 1771

It may therefore have a very happy effect if
whenever people introduce the subject [of eating
and drinking] you directly close, and push it home,
that they may understand a little more of this
important truth.

—JOHN WESLEY
"A Letter to a Friend, Concerning Tea," 1748

The most essential activity befitting humans created
in the image of God is to secure the food system
that God gives to sustain all creatures.

—ELLEN DAVIS
Scripture, Culture and Agriculture, 2009

AS WE HAVE seen, food ethics were not a mere afterthought for Wesley, but rather were central to his teachings
and doctrines. In Wesleyan thought, our food choices
matter immensely. Eating is not a morally neutral act.

Because he was convinced that God is interested in both our physical and spiritual well-being, Wesley worked to promote both "inward and outward health," believing that humanity has a duty to do as much as possible to preserve and restore the wellness God intends. As Randy Maddox says, "Wesley sees this life as a foretaste of what will be in the next. If the next life is to be a life of flourishing of body and soul, then in this life God also wants us to work toward a flourishing of body and soul, and that's what Wesley encouraged people to do."[1]

Wesley therefore called on his followers to exercise regularly and practice responsible, ethical diets. In fact, wellness and diet were central to Wesley's message in ways that might seem strange to churchgoers today, despite being as urgent and relevant as ever.

A Wesleyan Food Ethic, Made Plain

In his book *Serve God, Save the Planet*, Matthew Sleeth spells out a food ethic that John Wesley would endorse fully:

> [A] reason to abstain from food is if it was obtained through an immoral means—for instance, food that is stolen or gotten by child or slave labor. Additionally, God intends us to treat animals with respect. So food that is obtained from mistreated or tortured animals should be avoided. A third consideration is the consumption of food directly harmful to us. The Bible instructs us to care for our bodies as if they were temples of God (1 Corinthians 1:19). That's the rationale behind avoiding gluttony and drunkenness. Lastly our morals exclude us from eating food if the growing, harvesting, storing, or cooking of it is

harmful to others. This falls under the umbrella of the Golden Rule (Matthew 7:12). So at least four moral considerations exist that can call us to alter our diet. The first is a food shortage; the second is to avoid food obtained by unethical means; the third is to avoid food harmful to us; the last is to avoid food that causes harm to others.[2]

This is an ethic Wesleyans should claim as their own.

I submit that within Wesley's work it is possible to identify a seven-word food ethic, much like Michael Pollan's well-known "Eat food. Not too much. Mostly plants." While Wesley would emphatically agree that only nutritious food should be consumed, that vegetables should be favored over meat, and that food should be eaten in moderation, a Wesleyan food ethic would also strongly emphasize the importance of choosing food that has been produced ethically. Indeed, ethical production must be central in any truly Wesleyan food ethic. I suggest therefore that a Wesleyan food ethic, which may also be reduced to seven words, is: "Eat nutritious, ethically sourced food, in moderation."

Our ongoing cultural conversation about food, which the food movement has generated, would profit from the recovery of this ethic and its introduction into that conversation. And there should be a sense of urgency about that conversation. The diet that this industrial food system has generated and made possible is destroying our health. As a society, we are sinking under the weight of obesity and other illnesses caused by poor food choices, and we are complicit in an unsustainable food culture that is abusing animals, harming communities, and destroying creation. It is time for us to begin putting our faith into practice when we choose our food.

Are We Eating in Ways That Glorify God?

Wesley insisted that everything a Christian does in daily life, even "eating and sleeping, is prayer" and should be seen as worship and a means of glorifying God.[3] "To glorify him therefore with our bodies," he wrote, "as well as with our spirits; to go through our outward work with hearts lifted up to him; to make our daily employment a sacrifice to God; to buy and sell, to eat and drink, to his glory—that is worshipping God in spirit and in truth, as much as the praying to him in a wilderness."[4]

Elsewhere Wesley wrote that whatever a Methodist eats or drinks "tends to advance the glory of God, by peace and good-will among men."[5] But does eating eggs laid by a hen in a cage on a factory farm advance the glory of God? Does overeating to the point of obesity glorify God with our bodies? These are the kind of questions for which a Wesleyan food ethic would demand answers.

In Wesley's day his followers made a nutritious diet, moderation in eating, and attention to animal welfare essential elements of their religious practice, so much so that the general public, if asked to describe them, might well respond, "They take care of their health. They don't overeat. They care about the mistreatment of animals." Would those answers come to mind if someone was asked to describe a Wesleyan today? Probably not. Yet during the time Wesley was leading his Methodist revival, being a Methodist *meant*, among other things, those very things.

Christian Participation in the Food Movement

There is space in the food movement within which a Wesleyan food ethic could be articulated and appreciated.

Indeed, there is a vibrant Christian and Wesleyan presence in the movement. Some of the food movement's most prominent and influential leaders, such as Wendell Berry and Joel Salatin, are Christians who attribute their involvement, at least in part, to their faith. Numerous Christian entities and organizations, spanning the spectrum of American Christianity, have joined the call for better diets and a more sustainable food system. The United Church of Christ, for example, has created a curriculum titled "Just Eating," promoting healthy eating and food justice. Saddleback Church in California, Rick Warren's evangelical megachurch, implemented a health and wellness curriculum in 2011 that resulted in 15,000 church members losing more than 250,000 pounds. In December 2013, Warren released *The Daniel Plan: 40 Days to a Healthier Life*, coauthored with Drs. Daniel Amen and Mark Hyman, and it quickly became a *New York Times* best seller. First Presbyterian Church of Lexington, Kentucky, operates a 160-share CSA drawing from fifteen local farms while also providing food to local hunger-relief programs. The Wake Forest Divinity School recently launched a food and faith initiative and has created an MDiv program with a food emphasis. Liberty University has a campus garden, where students learn sustainable organic gardening skills. Episcopal priest Nurya Love Parish has produced a "Guide to the Christian Food Movement," and has led the way in creating a "Faith/Farm/Food network" aimed at "cultivating resilient communities through gardening and agriculture," and at working to "create a more just and sustainable food system which reflects the abundance and grace of God."[6] Dozens more examples could be easily cited. These and the many expressions like them reflect the fact that Christian communities are, in various ways and with

varying degrees of enthusiasm, embracing the food movement. While overall the church may be lagging behind,
there is an element of the food movement that is alive and
well across the full spectrum of American Christianity,
progressive and conservative.

These kinds of specifically Christian responses are
being welcomed and encouraged by leaders of the food
movement. Using his typically colorful language, farmer
and food movement advocate Joel Salatin, for example,
calls on American churches to embrace the food movement and make it central to their work:

> Lead by example. Turn church lawns into edible
> landscapes and gardens for parishioners to partici-
> pate in food production. Use church kitchens every
> day of the week to launch local food into commerce.
> Use the power of congregating to form alliances
> with local farmers for food pickups and distribution.
> Quit using Styrofoam at potlucks and quit assuming
> that if someone dares to pose these ideas they're a
> Democrat pagan Gaia worshipping Commie pinko
> liberal . . . Make food as important a ministry point
> as happy marriages, Bible study, financial coun-
> seling, and filling the missionary barrel.[7]

Christian authors are also beginning to look to the
food movement for ideas about how to revitalize Christian
faith. For example, Christopher Smith and John Pattison,
in their excellent and widely read 2014 book *Slow Church*,
call upon the contemporary church to consider how
Christian community could be strengthened and invigo-
rated by applying the principles embodied in the Slow
Food movement.[8] Likewise, in his book *Jesus, Bread and
Chocolate: Crafting a Hand-Made Faith in a Mass-Market
World*, John Thompson looks at the food movement,

but also more broadly at the surging appeal of "artisanal movements," evidenced by increasing appreciation of such things as locally grown food, hand-crafted specialty breads and chocolates, and home-brewed beer. Thompson sees in these movements a cultural yearning for high-quality, ethically produced alternatives to the industrialized, mass-produced products that are predominant in our culture (and that he sees reflected in many expressions of contemporary Christianity). He summons the church to reflect the values and ethics of these artisanal movements, rather than those of the industrialized economy.[9]

Wesleyan Participation in the Food Movement

Among Wesley's direct ecclesiological descendants, Methodists, Methodist churches, and Methodist institutions are actively participating in the movement as well, of course. Some of the prominent leaders of the environmental movement are Methodists, including Matthew Sleeth and Bill McKibben. During 2013, Queen Anne United Methodist Church in Seattle, Washington, hosted food movement luminaries Joel Salatin, Norman Wirzba, Bill McKibben, Marion Nestle, and others, as part of its speaker series.

Many Methodist churches have planted church gardens, such as the well-known Anathoth Community Garden in Cedar Grove, North Carolina. Another impressive example (from among many) is the Giving Garden at First United Methodist Church in Franklin, Tennessee, which produces more than a thousand pounds of produce each week for the needy in the community.

Methodist seminaries have also embraced the food movement in various ways. Duke Divinity School has an endowed chair devoted to food and rural life, currently held by food and faith theologian Norman Wirzba. Asbury Theological Seminary has a community garden. Both Duke and Asbury are founding members of the Seminary Stewardship Alliance, created by the Blessed Earth organization, which was founded by Methodists Matthew and Nancy Sleeth. The Methodist Theological School in Ohio has embraced ethical food initiatives with enthusiasm, incorporating food production into theological education in exciting ways, such as by offering degree programs focused on organic farming and food justice. The seminary even has its own organic farm on campus, which is the source of all the produce served in its dining hall. Food-based initiatives such as these are increasingly common, and numerous other examples could be cited.

Wesleyan scholars and pastors are also joining the discussion. Methodist pastor James Harnish in his book *Simple Rules for Money: John Wesley on Earning, Saving and Giving*, cited data demonstrating the accelerating obesity epidemic and issued a specific call for Christians to recognize their complicity in it.[10] Likewise, Methodist biblical scholar Ben Witherington devoted a chapter of his book *The Rest of Life* to a discussion of the obesity epidemic among American Christians and to a call for more responsible eating.[11] "We hear little or no teaching in the church about the ethical issues involved in eating and drinking," Witherington wrote. "Indeed eating seems to have been 'declassified' as an ethical issue among most modern Christians."[12]

Wesley scholar (and Free Methodist) Howard Snyder has long championed a Wesleyan environmental ethic. In his book *Salvation Means Creation Healed* (2011), Snyder implores Christians to connect their concern with creation care to the specific concerns of the food movement. He wrote, "Caring for creation means knowing the connection between the earth and our stomachs. Restoring food production to more healthy and sustainable forms of agriculture is part of the agenda of creation care. Healing creation means reforming the system."[13] He suggests forming "creation-affirming habits," such as moderate eating and regular exercise, and argues that industrial agricultural monocultures are inconsistent with the Christian vision of healing, restoration, and reversal of the effects of the Fall.[14] Snyder recommends nine specific practices to promote the discipline of creation care, one of which is to "eat locally as much as possible."

> Buying and eating locally helps heal the land while improving our own health. Consider the benefits: 1) fresher, more nutritious, and better tasting food; 2) less ingestion of unknown and unneeded chemicals, artificial flavors and coloring, and obesity-inducing high fructose corn syrup; 3) reduction in the fossil fuels and pollution involved in shipping food around the world; 4) encouragement of the local economy. Supporting the local economy is an act of social justice; a revolutionary act of resistance against the unhealthy industrialization of our food supply. It reinforces the growing movement toward healthier, more sustainable local and global economies.[15]

In 2013 Jennifer Ayres, professor of religious education at the Candler School of Theology, an official United Methodist seminary, published her book *Good Food: Grounded Practical Theology*, in which she examined both the nature and consequences of the global food system and various Christian responses to it. Drawing upon the theological implications of the Eucharist meal, she advocates a "grounded theology" oriented around four moral commitments rooted in food practices: "prioritization of the hungry, solidarity with an advocacy for those who work the land, the call to care gently for the land, and the reestablishment of bonds of interdependence between humans and the sources of our food."[16]

The Social Principles of the United Methodist Church also affirm many of the priorities of the food movement. They call specifically, for example, for "policies that encourage and support a gradual transition to sustainable and organic agriculture." They recognize the value of family farms, calling for "a sustainable agricultural system . . . where agricultural animals are treated humanely and where their living conditions are as close to natural systems as possible," and they encourage Methodists to "practice or support organic gardening." A resolution adopted in 2008 cited Wesley's concern for health and wellness and identified "overeating or eating nonnutritious foods" as among those personal lifestyle factors detrimental to health, urging Methodists to "work for policies that enable people to . . . eat wholesome food," and calling upon churches to "accept responsibility for educating and motivating members to follow a healthy lifestyle reflecting our affirmation of life as God's gift." A resolution titled "Health and Wholeness" provides: "The biblical mandate has specific implications for personal care. We must honor our bodies through exercise. We must honor our bodies through proper nutrition, and reducing consumption of food products that we discover add toxins to our bodies, excess weight to our frames, and yet fail to provide nourishment. We must recognize that honoring our bodies is a lifelong process." The resolution notes that "habits or addictions destructive to good health include overeating or eating nonnutritious foods," and calls upon Methodists to "make health concerns a priority in the church."[17]

If a Wesleyan food ethic is to emerge within the American church, clearly the seeds for it are already being planted.

Why Are Food Ethics Usually Absent from the Church?

In light of Wesley's clear, consistent, and repeated teachings on these matters, the centrality of them to his overall message, and the leading role being played by Wesleyans within the Christian component of the food movement, why aren't these healthy practices being broadly reflected within the church? Why is the church no healthier than the public at large, and perhaps even worse off?

For one thing, there does not seem to be any consistently accepted food ethic evident in the American church at large. While there are a few voices shedding theological light on the subject of food, there is at present no twenty-first-century equivalent of John Wesley. Further, judging from the obesity data, churchgoers are more likely to make poor food choices than those who do not attend church, and pastors are even more likely than their congregations. If there is indeed a Christian moral obligation to eat only nutritious food, and to eat in moderation, it seems fair to say that by and large that moral obligation is being disregarded.

Certainly part of the problem may be a prevailing belief, albeit a decidedly non-Wesleyan one, that spiritual and religious matters relate only to things of the soul and are unconcerned with the physical body. Yet while this may be a factor for some, it has not prevented Christians from making spiritual issues of sexuality and (historically) alcohol and tobacco use, for example. It seems more likely therefore that the lack of attention to human health and wellness in the church is attributable to the fact that overeating and poor food choices are simply now culturally accepted and are typically no longer regarded as vices or moral shortcomings.

How likely is a pastor to deliver a sermon challenging overeating as sinful when a third or more of his congregation are obese? How often can such sermons be expected when nearly half of the pastors themselves are obese? How likely is a pastor to condemn concentrated animal agriculture and processed foods before a congregation whose favorite restaurant is Chick-fil-A and who will in large part head to places like KFC after church? Yet, can there be any doubt that John Wesley would preach such sermons?

And if gluttony is no longer considered a vice, what cost might that have to the overall well-being of the church? How can pastors who are themselves seemingly unable to control the most basic of appetites, expect to be taken seriously when teaching their congregations that they should exercise self-control in other areas of their lives?

Recovering the Wesleyan Food Ethic

The time is right to recover the Wesleyan food ethic and to restore it to the central place it once occupied in Wesleyan thought. We live in a culture that regularly promotes poor food choices and attaches no moral stigma to them. As we have seen, studies show that regular church-going people are more likely to make poor food choices (and suffer the resulting health consequences) than non-churchgoers. And pastors tend to be worse about it than their congregations. This is a major disconnect from traditionally accepted teachings of the church. As on so many things, John Wesley's centuries-old teachings speak directly into our culture's food choice failings. Again, from Randy Maddox: "Wesley was concerned not just about how we heal that which is sick or broken but also how we nurture sustaining practices of health. He stressed that we ought to practice proper diet, exercise, and sleep in order to cultivate health, that God created and sustains us, and expects this of us."[18] This is a message that our culture, and specifically the church, desperately needs to hear. Thanks to the food movement and the Christian/Wesleyan participation in it, the platform for advancing this message is already in place.

Of course, we must resist the temptation to see John Wesley as a twenty-first-century authority on nutrition, medicine, exercise, animal welfare, or similar matters. Rather, he was an eighteenth-century evangelist, and while he has left an important ecclesiological legacy, his teachings should not be used merely as a proof-texting resource for the promotion of contemporary social policies. That is not to say, however, that Wesley's views are without any importance. The undeniable fact is that Wesley has left an immense and significant theological and ecclesiological legacy, and that millions of Christians continue to have their faith and their lives shaped and informed by his teachings. Arguably, to obtain the full beneficial impact of those teachings, it is critical that they be maintained and preserved in context of all of Wesley's thought. If some noteworthy portion of Wesley's teachings is being neglected or ignored, then there is a genuine risk that those teachings that are being preserved are incomplete or insufficient in material ways, and are therefore delivering less benefit than a holistic appreciation of Wesley's work would confer.

Put directly, Wesley would never separate his teachings on the importance of health, nutritious food, temperance, and the proper treatment of animals from the balance of his teachings. Instead, he would insist that attention to only part of his message, and neglect of some other part, would have the effect of distorting his teaching and failing to deliver that which he intended.

The word *Wesleyan* should call to mind, among other things, an ethic regarding nutritious food, moderation in eating, the humane and compassionate treatment of animals, and a just and ethical food system, just as it once did. One cannot claim and adhere to an authentic holistic Wesleyan theology while ignoring, disregarding, or willfully rejecting Wesley's teachings on food. It is possible to adhere to a Wesleyan food ethic without being Wesleyan, but it is not possible to be fully Wesleyan without adhering to the Wesleyan food ethic.

For Christians in Wesleyan traditions, the food movement is part of their ecclesiastical DNA. In no other segment of mainstream American Christianity do issues of health, wellness, and food justice historically figure so centrally. The food movement is alive, well, and thriving in our culture. For contemporary Wesleyans to infuse that movement with a theological foundation as old as their tradition itself (indeed, a foundation that was once at the very core of that tradition), it would not be a case of getting on board with the latest secular cultural trend or fashion statement. Rather, it should be seen as reconnecting with an ethic deeply embedded in the faith tradition, which has been lost to culture and its emphasis on industrialization and overconsumption. And the resulting harvest might be marvelous.

If Wesley's food ethic were recovered and made a central part of the teachings of the Methodist and Wesleyan churches, perhaps Wesleyans could take leading roles in the efforts to reverse the obesity epidemic, end or reform the factory farm/CAFO system, and ensure a safe, reliable, equitable, and sustainable food system. If so, John Wesley would surely be pleased.

And importantly, it is not just modern-day Wesleyans who stand to benefit from attention to a Wesleyan food ethic. Recovery of the historic Wesleyan food ethic might be profitable not only to those in Wesleyan traditions, but to all Christians who are looking for a point of entry into our ongoing cultural conversation about food that is grounded in faith and in the history and tradition of the church. Indeed, an ethic that explicitly defines good food as that which is nutritious, eaten in moderation, and ethically sourced, should resonate broadly among those of all backgrounds, whether Christian or not, who are looking for a way to engage the food movement that is motivated not only by a desire for personal well-being and pleasure, but also by a desire to improve the world, help others, and honor the Creator.

Of course, Wesley's teachings about food must be seen and considered within the context of his larger call to a cultivation of personal and social holiness and a striving toward the perfection that God intends. So while Wesley taught that disciplined ethical eating was a means of obedience to God and part of the cultivation of personal holiness, he was not merely some sort of food Pharisee. He did not call upon his followers simply to obey a list of rules about eating. Rather, he encouraged them to eat in ways that would contribute not only to their personal health, but also to the betterment of the world, celebrating the goodness of creation in life-affirming ways, while advancing God's kingdom and glory. Just as Wesley could state matter-of-factly that a Methodist does not sell things that are harmful to the health of others, he also emphasized that we must consider who bears the consequences of our purchases, such as the poor who suffer as a result of overconsumption by the wealthy. Wesley understood that the food God has provided for humanity should be used to keep us nourished and healthy, for God's service. Thus we should never gratify our desires with gluttony, at the expense of not only our own health, but the poor, and God's creation. The need for such a food ethic is no less urgent today than it was in Wesley's time, and indeed may be more important now than ever.

Given how broadly our society has now been infected by the consequences of poor food choices and the power of the industrial food complex, recovering the Wesleyan ethic will not be easy. We must remain mindful that criticism of the system and its effects may be perceived as criticism of those who are suffering from those effects. If the Wesleyan ethic is to be recovered, therefore, let it be introduced gently and lovingly, to inform, guide, and bless people; not to shame, ridicule, or condemn them. Millions of people have been lured gradually and unsuspectingly into an unethical and health-destroying food culture. We cannot reasonably expect them to be drawn out of it overnight. But while a sincere desire to avoid producing shame or guilt in those who are suffering the consequences of poor food choices should inform our discussion, it must not silence it. There is too much at stake.

A modern-day Wesley would, no doubt, find much to criticize about the industrial food system and our society's food choices. In one sense, the contemporary food movement is a vehicle for such critiques. Importantly, however, the movement is also a vehicle through which the goodness of God and nature can be praised and celebrated. Thus, while we might expect a modern-day Wesley to join the movement in its fight against the industrial food system, we should also expect that with equal passion he would join it in embracing and celebrating life-sustaining food, vigorously healthy bodies, contented farm animals, and benevolent community-based economies.

Wesleyan teaching recognizes that our choices about such things as what we eat have ripple effects on all of creation. If we ruin our health by eating poorly, we disable ourselves from doing good. If we eat too much, we take food off the plates of those who are hungry. If we buy or sell items that are harmful to us or to others, then we are spreading harm rather than preventing it. For Wesley, making morally correct decisions about food is far more important than just obeying rules and trying to win divine favor. By making the right choices, we synch our lives with God's will for the world, thus living into the new creation and being a part of God's renewal and restoration of all things.

Doing Good by Eating Well

Wesley called upon Christians to "do all the good thou canst." For Wesley, doing good—in all things and to the greatest extent possible—is an essential characteristic of a properly lived Christian life.

From a Wesleyan perspective, eating (like everything else we do) is an opportunity to do good. When we

choose nutritious ethically-produced food and consume
it in moderation, we do good for our bodies, we do good
for our neighbors and communities, we do good for our
fellow creatures, we do good for the environment, and we
do good for all of creation. Nutritious ethically-produced
food is *good* food.

"He is already renewing
the face of the earth."

Wesley expected that his Methodist revival would
spread from heart to heart and house to house, gradually
covering the whole land, ushering in and leaving in its
wake God's restored creation. "All unprejudiced persons
may see with their eyes that he is already renewing the
face of the earth," he wrote.[19] He might be disappointed
to see that more than 250 years later the transformation
he anticipated has not yet occurred. But no doubt Wesley
would continue to trust that people renewed and invigo-
rated by his call could still initiate such a process. In fact,
Wesley might well see the food movement as an opportunity to introduce into the broader cultural conversation
his message of spiritual renewal. As he put it in his 1748
"Letter to a Friend, Concerning Tea," "Neither is there
any need that conversation should be unedifying, even
when it turns upon eating and drinking. Nay, from such
a conversation, if duly improved numberless good effects
may flow . . . It may therefore have a very happy effect if
whenever people introduce the subject you directly close,
and push it home, that they may understand a little more
of this important truth." Wesley leaves no doubt of the
importance and potential benefit he placed on conversation that "turns upon eating and drinking." As our society

is engaged in just such a conversation these days, the time is right to "directly close" and "push home" a Wesleyan food ethic, from which "numberless good effects may flow."[20]

Looking back over the centuries at John Wesley, we can determine where his views situated him in his culture. But more important, we can evaluate how those views might inform behavior today, particularly among those whose behavior is already otherwise significantly informed by Wesley's teachings. The fact of the matter is that Wesley's teachings align with the principal values of the contemporary food movement. This significant and growing social movement would resonate with Wesley, and it should therefore resonate with those for whom Wesley's teachings are meaningful. A Wesleyan food ethic is already present in the food movement, but it is there anonymously. Now seems an ideal time to unveil it, and especially to reintroduce it to the Wesleyan communities who have forgotten it.

For Discussion

1. What do you think it means to eat ethically? Are there moral implications in choosing what and how much to eat?

2. In your community, do those who regularly attend church seem to be healthier than those who do not? Are their diets any different from those of the unchurched? What do your answers to these questions suggest?

3. What do you think about the suggestion that there is a specifically identifiable Wesleyan food ethic? Are you persuaded that Wesley's teachings contain such an ethic? Have you ever seen any evidence of it in your church?

4. If Wesley's teachings on food were more well-known, do you think they might have an impact on how Wesleyans and other Christians perceive the food movement? Might they have an impact on how the food movement perceives Wesleyans and other Christians?

5. Would you like to hear about food ethics in your church? If Wesley's teachings on food were better known, what effect might they have?

10

Living the Ethic

All that a Christian does, even in eating and sleeping, is prayer, when it is done in simplicity, according to the order of God.

—JOHN WESLEY
A Plain Account of Christian Perfection, 1738

The surest way to escape the Western diet is simply to depart the realms it rules: the supermarket, the convenience store, and the fast food outlet.

—MICHAEL POLLAN
Food Rules, 2009

SO NOW WHAT? If you are persuaded that you should try to incorporate a Wesleyan food ethic into your life, then naturally the next question is how best to do that. It may seem intimidating. Our culture bombards us daily with messages and incentives designed to lead us to poor food choices. In our hectic, busy lives, it is only natural to take advantage of convenience whenever we can. And, of course, we may have a lifetime of tastes and eating habits that won't be easy to change. But the good news is that beginning the journey of living into this ethic is much easier than it may seem on the surface, and does not usually require drastic and immediate changes to our daily lives. This chapter will suggest some of the ways to begin incorporating an ethic of good food into our lives—an ethic that can be an important part not only of affirming and sustaining life, but of having life more abundantly.

You Don't Have to Do it All at Once

Perhaps you've decided to plow up your backyard, plant a garden, become a vegan, and eat nothing but home-grown organic food the rest of your life. If so, that's great. Godspeed. But for most of us that kind of immediate, radical change is not practical. If forced to choose between that kind of lifestyle change and continuing to eat badly, many of us would choose the latter.

Don't be put off, however, by the notion that eating well will necessarily require such immediate, drastic changes in your life. Where we recognize the need to change our diets, we can begin making these changes without making them all at once. The first steps are simply acknowledging the importance of eating ethically, identifying those areas in our lives and diets that need change, then implementing those changes in a way and at a pace that keeps us encouraged to continue moving forward, rather than setting us up for a sense of failure.

Neither should we be discouraged by the fear that eating better will make us unhappy. Many people wrongly assume that eating well means self-deprivation, such as never again eating dessert, having to permanently give up favorite foods, or feeling hungry all the time. But in fact, as many who have begun this journey can attest, people who replace unhealthy diets with nutritious and ethically sourced food tend not only to be healthier, but also to feel better and to appreciate and enjoy food more than they ever have before. The image of a healthy ethical eater as a sour monkish figure, subsisting on lentils and carrot sticks, simply does not match the reality of a life enriched by enjoying the pleasures and satisfaction that come from good food. Chances are you know someone who is cheerfully living a healthy lifestyle, and who enjoys a diet of good food. Look to that person for inspiration, rather than to food snobs or some stereotype you may have in mind. Remember too that if you are persuaded that a diet of ethically sourced nutritious food, eaten in moderation, is part of God's desire for your life, then you should expect God's favor and blessing as you sincerely, diligently, and prayerfully seek to make the necessary changes in your life. If you ask for a fish, you will not be given a snake.

Be Mindful and Prayerful

As with all things in life, changing the way we eat is not something we should try to do alone. A Wesleyan food ethic rests on the foundation that it is God's will and desire that we nourish our bodies with healthy food, that we eat no more than is necessary to maintain our health, and that in choosing our food we remain mindful of the consequences our choices have not only for ourselves, but for the rest of creation as well. We should choose this ethic out of a committed belief that following it will better honor God and better reflect God's desire for us and the rest of creation—that we be healthy and that our food choices contribute to making the world a better place.

As Wesley taught, nothing is separate from God, and everything we do, including eating, should be thought of as prayer. In that sense, of course, we should always be in prayer. But beyond that, I suggest two specific, intentional manners of prayer that will be beneficial as we seek to make the Wesleyan food ethic a part of our everyday lives: (1) that we prayerfully and mindfully choose our food, and (2) that we prayerfully consume it in a spirit of thanksgiving.

In his sermon "On the Use of Money," Wesley called upon Christians to carefully and deliberately pray about every expenditure of money, including specifically money spent on food. He suggests four questions that should be prayerfully asked of every potential purchase:

> If, then, a doubt should at any time arise in your mind concerning what you are going to expend, either on yourself or any part of your family, you have an easy way to remove it. Calmly and seriously inquire, "(1) In expending this, am I acting according to my character? Am I acting herein, not as a proprietor, but as a steward of my Lord's goods? (2) Am I doing this in obedience to his Word? In what Scripture does he require me so to do? (3) Can I offer up this action, this expense, as a sacrifice to God through Jesus Christ? (4) Have I reason to believe that for this very work I shall have a reward at the resurrection of the just?" You will seldom need anything more to remove any doubt which arises on this head; but by this four-fold consideration you will receive clear light as to the way wherein you should go.
>
> If any doubt still remain, you may farther examine yourself by prayer according to those heads of inquiry. Try whether you can say to the Searcher of hearts, your conscience not condemning you, "Lord, thou seest I am going to expend this sum on that food, apparel, furniture. And thou knowest, I act herein with a single eye as a steward of thy goods, expending this portion of them thus

in pursuance of the design thou hadst in entrusting me with them. Thou knowest I do this in obedience to the Lord, as thou commandest, and because thou commandest it. Let this, I beseech thee, be an holy sacrifice, acceptable through Jesus Christ! And give me a witness in myself that for this labour of love I shall have a recompense when thou rewardest every man according to his works." Now if your conscience bear you witness in the Holy Ghost that this prayer is well-pleasing to God, then have you no reason to doubt but that expense is right and good, and such as will never make you ashamed.

In our contemporary food culture, where making poor food choices is so easy, convenient, and tempting, we would do well to bear Wesley's questions and suggested prayer in mind when choosing our food. Recast in contemporary language, we might ask:

1. In choosing this food am I being a good steward of both my money and my body?
2. In choosing this food am I being disobedient to God by doing harm to my body, by being gluttonous, or by contributing to the mistreatment of animals or of the poor?
3. Is this food worthy to be offered as a sacrifice to God?
4. In choosing this food am I participating in God's redemption and restoration of creation, or am I being complicit in its destruction?

If we follow Wesley's advice to consider those questions calmly, honestly, seriously, and prayerfully, we should expect that our food choices will always be "right and good, such as will never make you ashamed."

In addition to being prayerful when we choose our food, we should be prayerful when eating it as well. In his sermon "The More Excellent Way," Wesley taught that people should pray earnestly at mealtimes, rather than just offering up some perfunctory prayer from habit. He called upon people to pray both before and after eating, first asking God's blessing on the food, and then, after eating it, to "return thanks to the Giver of all his blessings." This, he said, would be "a more excellent way."

As we seek a more excellent way of eating, we should remain mindful that our food, like our health, is a gift of God. By stopping to earnestly ask God's blessing on our food before we eat it, we give ourselves an opportunity to reflect on both the quality and quantity of what we are about to consume. We should prayerfully consider whether what we are about to eat honors God and creation in such a way that it merits God's blessing. And by pausing after our meals to return thanks to God, we allow ourselves time to reflect on whether we have used God's gift of food well. Considering the food we have eaten, do we feel led to offer a prayer of thanksgiving for God's provision, or do we feel the need to ask forgiveness?

These prayer practices can assist us on our journey to diets that are characterized by nutritious, ethically sourced food, and they can help us overcome addiction to overeating. In Paul's letter to the Galatians he lists self-control as among the fruit of the Spirit, along with love, joy, peace, kindness, goodness, faithfulness, gentleness, and forbearance. As we make the dietary changes to which we feel called, let us not neglect to cultivate the fruit of the Spirit, and use the self-control that God has given us.

For Almost All of Us, Eating Better Is Not Unaffordable

Far too many people resist making changes to their diets because they wrongly believe they cannot afford to eat healthy food. Yet for the vast majority of us, as shown in chapter 8, this is a myth. As a society we now spend less of our disposable income on food than any society in world history. By and large, we have more than enough money to be able to afford healthy food; it's just that we live in a society that has artificially elevated the importance of nonfood expenditures, causing us to believe that many luxuries are in fact necessities.

Of course, as we saw in chapter 8, Wesley taught and believed that there was nothing more important on which to spend money than a diet of simple, health-sustaining food. Out of every hundred dollars of disposable income, the average American household spends less than ten dollars on food. Before concluding that there is no money left in the budget for healthier food, it would be wise to first examine what the other ninety-plus dollars of our income is being spent on, and whether or not those expenditures are improving our health and the world around us. Many of us will discover that we can easily afford to improve the quality of our food if we spend fewer of our dollars on less important (and often harmful) things.

Before concluding that healthy food is unaffordable, we should also make sure we are properly comparing apples to apples. For example, a bag of organic potato chips may be more expensive than a bag of ordinary potato chips. But making that switch would simply be replacing one unhealthy snack food with another (albeit somewhat less unhealthy) one. A better comparison would be the price of potato chips versus the price of potatoes. With the former you are paying mostly for packaging and getting very little food, whereas potatoes themselves, even organic ones, are relatively inexpensive.

Frozen vegetables are usually inexpensive and nearly as nutritious as fresh produce. In fact, frozen vegetables in a supermarket are often more nutritious than the "fresh" produce sold there, which may well have been picked weeks ago. Likewise, nutritious and tasty whole foods, such as dried beans and rice, are inexpensive and can become the foundations for delicious, wholesome meals. For many people, eliminating calorie-rich, nutrient-poor processed foods from their diets and replacing them with nutritious whole foods, will actually cause their food expenditures to *decrease*. Remember also that it is not necessary to buy all of your food from expensive, upscale, specialty grocery stores in order to eat a healthy diet.

In some cases, though, eating ethically will make it necessary to spend more money on some kinds of food. For example, chocolate that is not certified fair trade is often produced using the labor of child slaves in Africa. To eat ethically, and to avoid being complicit in this, you may need to buy only certified fair trade chocolate, which is usually more expensive. But if you purchase chocolate only as an occasional treat, and eat it in small quantities, you should be able to continue to enjoy chocolate without having to increase your overall food budget. By doing so, not only will your chocolate purchases no longer generate profits for slaveholders, but by eating less highly processed chocolate candy, your health will benefit as well. Likewise, fair trade coffee and tea are more expensive than conventional varieties. But the cost per cup is not significantly greater and is a cost worth bearing to help be a part of ending the exploitation of workers and farmers on coffee and tea plantations.

Eggs and meat from humanely raised animals also tend to be more expensive than those from animals raised in factory farm CAFOs. But by reducing the amount of meat in our diets, we should be able to afford ethically produced meat without increasing the overall amount spent on meat. Nutrition experts agree that as a society we eat too much meat. Indeed, modern science has borne out Wesley's belief that a plant-based diet, low in meat, is the most conducive to good health. Studies link diets high in vegetables and low in meat to lower rates of cancer, heart disease, diabetes, and other serious illnesses. So instead of a regular diet of chicken nuggets and cheeseburgers, why don't we instead turn to a plant-based diet, enjoying only an occasional pastured chicken, pasture-raised pork, or beef from grass-fed cattle? Here again it is possible to eat more ethically, without spending more money.

Likewise, eggs from free-range hens are more expensive than eggs from hens living in battery cages. But for the price of a dozen farm-fresh, ethically produced eggs from a local farm a person can have breakfast for a week and still spend less than the cost of a large bag of Doritos and a Mountain Dew. If we consider whether the cost of ethical food is reasonable, as opposed to merely comparing it to the price of industrial food, we may well conclude that it is not as expensive as we once believed.

Obviously there are some who cannot afford even a minimal increase in the cost of their food, even though they are not overeating or wasting money on expensive, health-impairing junk food. Wesley repeatedly emphasized that those of us who can do so have a Christian duty to come to the aid of those who are unable to afford healthy food for themselves and their families. As much as anything else, this is an integral component of a Wesleyan food ethic.

Avoid Processed Foods and Favor Whole Foods, Cooked at Home Whenever Possible

Replacing processed foods with nutritious whole foods is probably the single most important step toward a healthier diet. Sometimes the difference between the two will be obvious. Everyone knows that an apple is a whole food while a Twinkie is a processed food. Fresh and frozen fruits, vegetables, and meats are whole foods. Food products that are prepackaged and made from ingredients that are found in factories or chemical laboratories but not in any normal kitchen (such as the ingredients in nearly all snack foods) are processed foods. When in doubt, read the label. If the product contains ingredients you don't recognize as food, then it is almost certainly a processed food. Remember Michael Pollan's advice: if the ingredient lists include things that would not be in a typical kitchen pantry and that a third grader probably couldn't pronounce, the food shouldn't be a significant part of your diet.

In our busy lives we often feel too rushed to prepare meals at home, so we increasingly rely on fast-food outlets for our nourishment. But of course eating greasy fast foods and drinking sugary drinks in our cars is a recipe for a health disaster and makes us complicit in the animal abuse and environmental degradation that underlie the fast-food industry. For those of us who have fallen into the fast-food trap, perhaps by consciously striving to adopt a Wesleyan food ethic we can begin the process of weaning ourselves from that kind of food. Then we can replace it with good food that will sustain rather than damage our health, and that has been produced using methods that align with our morals, rather than conflict with them.

One good way to start would be to make it a practice to have at least one family meal each day, made from whole foods prepared at home. Some have found that dividing the responsibility for meal preparation (and cleaning up afterward) among family members is a good way to lessen the burden that might otherwise fall on only one person, while teaching the skills and joys of cooking. Consider what works best for your family, but try to make time in the day for at least one meal that is not rushed and is enjoyed with family.

Wherever Possible, Find and Support Local, Trustworthy Sources of Food

The best way to assure that the food you are eating has been produced ethically is to get as much of it as you can from sources you personally know and trust. If possible, plant a garden and get a few chickens. If not, consider keeping a few tomato plants (or any other favorite vegetable) in containers. Growing at least some of your own food will not only give you a source of fresh, delicious, ethically produced food; it will help reconnect you to the beauties and joys of growing food—a connection that has been fundamental to human existence from the beginning, but is now imperiled by the industrial food system.

Most communities now have farmers' markets, where you can find fresh, seasonal, locally grown food. And by supporting local farmers you will help keep your local food economy alive and resilient. Most farmers enjoy the opportunity to talk about their farming practices, so you should be able easily to find local farms that operate in accordance with your food ethic. Localharvest.org is a good resource as well. At that site, by entering your zip code, you can pull up a list of farms in your community, identifying what they offer and how their food is produced. To find meat and eggs from animals raised humanely and naturally, it is particularly important to try to find local farms whose practices are transparent.

Eat Less, Exercise More

Much of the health crisis we are experiencing in our culture today comes from eating too much and exercising too little. Too much food and too little exercise creates an unhealthy imbalance in our lives. In the simplest terms, if we consume more calories than we burn, we will become obese and unhealthy. Most of us must correct the imbalance by reducing the amount we eat (particularly unhealthy processed food) and increasing the amount of exercise we get.

As discussed in chapter 4, throughout his ministry Wesley repeatedly emphasized the necessity of sufficient exercise and moderation in eating. Our bodies, Wesley said, are gifts from God and we are merely stewards of them. We therefore have an obligation to preserve our health and treat our bodies well. By doing so we are not only being obedient to God, but we are also keeping ourselves fit for whatever purposes God may have for us.

Once moderate eating and reasonable exercise become habits, they will not seem burdensome to us. To get started, Wesley would insist that we should look to God for strength and call upon the self-control that is a fruit of the Spirit.

Share

Like all the practices and disciplines of our faith, eating ethically and living the Wesleyan food ethic is something that is best done in community, not in isolation. For those who are about to begin this journey, consider traveling together with your family, small group, or congregation, helping and supporting each other along the way by sharing advice, encouragement, discoveries, challenges, and concerns. It is likely that some of the changes you will want to make will not come easy. Having others traveling along the way with you may help you through the times when you are discouraged or uncertain how to proceed. Likewise, if you are well established in the practice of ethical eating and are in a position to help those who are not so far along, consider becoming a mentor, sharing with them your experiences and practical tips that make the journey easier.

Imagine

For most of us it will be easy to imagine the benefits that will come from eating better. We may imagine losing weight and feeling better, becoming healthy enough to no longer need as many medications, and living longer, more fulfilling lives. Of course these are all excellent reasons for choosing to eat a healthier diet. But the Wesleyan vision is grander than that.

Imagine a world in which all of humanity eats only ethically produced nutritious food, in moderation. In such a world there would be less sickness, less disease, no gluttony, and a population living long, healthy lives. Farm animals would be raised naturally and compassionately, being afforded the respect they deserve as beloved creatures of God. There would be no exploitation of farm workers and farmers. The land would be treated gently and respectfully, with farming practices that ensure a sustainable, resilient, regenerative future. There would be robust and vibrant community-based food economies.

In such a world, the food system would be a part of God's renewal and restoration of creation, rather than an impediment to it.

May it be so.

Let our next meal, and all those that follow it, be a part of bringing that vision to reality.

For Discussion

1. Are you persuaded of the importance of Wesley's food ethic? Why or why not?

2. What specific changes do you intend to make in your family's diet? What benefits do you expect to see from those changes?

3. What are some of the obstacles to eating better? How will we find the time to prepare more meals at home and eat them together as a family? Will it cost more? Can we afford it?

4. The author asks us to imagine a world in which all people follow Wesley's food ethic. Can you imagine what the world will look like if no one follows the ethic? What will be the consequences to future generations?

5. Did you learn anything from this book? Does it leave you wanting to learn more? If so, how might you do that?

Appendix

Here are some resources to help you on your journey to ethical eating. This is just a small sampling of the excellent resources that are now available, but these are good starting points from which to begin the journey.

For more about **the industrial food system and the countervailing food movement**, the documentaries "Food, Inc." and "Fresh" are excellent introductions. Also, "Farmland" is a worthwhile, balanced, industry-sponsored film that includes sympathetic perspectives from industrial farmers.

Among books, Michael Pollan's writing is engaging and continues to be influential. *In Defense of Food: An Eater's Manifesto* (Penguin, 2008) and *The Omnivore's Dilemma: A Natural History of Four Meals* (Penguin, 2006) are informative and entertaining. Eric Schlosser's classic *Fast Food Nation: The Dark Side of the All-American Meal* (Houghton Mifflin, 2001) is still relevant and eye-opening. Less well-known, but one of the best examinations of our food culture and, most importantly, the power of the consumer to change it, is Ellen Gustafson's *We the Eaters: If We Change Dinner We Can Change the World* (Rodale, 2014).

For useful tips on how **to begin growing food on a small scale**, the website http://squarefootgardening.org/ and the corresponding book *Square Foot Gardening: A New*

Way to Garden in Less Space with Less Work by Mel Bartholomew (Rodale, 2005) are highly recommended.

To **find ethically-produced locally-grown food**, locate the farmers markets in your community by using the USDA's farmer's market search page at http://search.ams.usda.gov /farmersmarkets/. Likewise, if you search the term "find local farmer's market" on Google, the first result will be your nearest farmers market. http://www.localharvest.org/ is another excellent resource. Just type in your zip code and you'll be given a list of area farms and their products.

You can **learn to read food labels and search for nutritional information** about foods at http://nutritiondata .self.com/. Remember that whenever possible you should choose whole, natural foods and avoid highly processed foods.

Smart phone apps that assist in shopping for ethical food are increasingly available. You can find some examples at http://ecowatch.com/2015/02/23/apps-sustainable-food -shopping/.

The Rev. Nurya Love Parish has assembled resources related to the **Christian Food Movement** in her *Guide to the Christian Food Movement*, which may be downloaded free through her Churchwork website: http://www .churchwork.com/christian-food-movement/.

Notes

Introduction

1. Wendell Berry, *Bringing It to the Table: On Farming and Food* (Berkeley: Counterpoint, 2009), x.

Chapter 1

1. Beginning with this section and continuing throughout the book, numerous agricultural and health data are presented without citations to avoid an overabundance of endnotes. The data comes primarily from the following four sources:

   The Centers for Disease Control and Prevention: www.cdc.gov

   USDA Economic Research Services: http://www .ers.usda.gov/publications

   USDA National Agricultural Statistics Service: http://www.nass.usda.gov/

   USDA National Conservation Research Service: http://www.nrcs.usda.gov/

2. Carrie Hirbar, *Understanding Concentrated Animal Feeding Operations and Their Impact on Communities* (Bowling Green, OH: National Association of Local Boards of Health, 2010), 1; http://www.cdc.gov/nceh /ehs/docs/understanding_cafos_nalboh.pdf.

3. Paul Conkin, *A Revolution Down on the Farm: The Transformation of American Agriculture Since 1929* (Lexington, KY: University Press of Kentucky, 2008), 152.

4. Bill McKibben, *Deep Economy: The Wealth of Communities and the Durable Future* (New York: Times Books, 2007), 52–53.

5. Ibid, 54–55.

6. Quoted in Michael Moss, *Salt Sugar Fat: How the Food Giants Hooked Us* (New York: Random House, 2013), xvii.

7. Michael Moss, "The Extraordinary Science of Addictive Junk Food," *New York Times Magazine*, February 20, 2013.

8. Michael Pollan, *Food Rules: An Eater's Manual* (London: Penguin, 2009), xii–xiv. See also Melanie Warner, *Pandora's Lunchbox: How Processed Foods Took Over the American Meal* (New York: Scribner, 2013), 66–67, for a discussion of some of the findings of research examining the link.

9. Ellen Gustafson, *We the Eaters: If We Change Dinner We Can Change the World* (New York: Rodale, 2014), xv.

10. See, for example, Michael Pollan, *Food Rules*; Pollan, *The Omnivore's Dilemma: The Natural History of Four Meals* (London: Penguin, 2006); Pollan, *In Defense of Food: An Eater's Manifesto* (London: Penguin, 2008); and Barbara Kingsolver, *Animal, Vegetable, Miracle: A Year of Food Life* (New York: HarperCollins, 2007). These are among the best known, but there are many other popular titles with similar themes.

Chapter 2

1. Wesley's sermons, journals, and other writings are now extensively available, both online and in print. My principal source for Wesley's writings was the Baker Book House's 1986 reprint of the 1872 edition of *The Works of John Wesley*, 3rd, ed. edited by Thomas Jackson, originally issued by the Wesleyan Methodist Book Room, London. I also used the resources

available at Northwest Nazarene University's Wesley
Center Online (http://wesley.nnu.edu/), where much
of Wesley's work is collected, as well as materials
available in the online resources of the B. L. Fisher
Library of Asbury Theological Seminary and in the
online resources of the library of the Duke Divinity
School. To avoid cluttering the book with endnotes,
citations to the Wesley source documents are only
provided when the context does not make the source
evident.

2. William Abraham, "Wesley as Preacher," *Cambridge
Companion to John Wesley*, ed. Randy L. Maddox and
Jason E. Vickers (New York: Cambridge University
Press, 2010), 98.

3. For more on Cheyne's life and background, see
H. Newton Malony, "John Wesley's Primitive Physick,"
Journal of Health Psychology 1, no. 2 (1996), 150.

4. George Cheyne, *An Essay on Regimen: Together with
Five Discourses, Medical, Moral, and Philosophical:
Serving to Illustrate the Principles and Theory of
Philosophical Medicine, and Point Out Some of Its
Moral Consequences* (London: printed for C. Rivington
and J. Leake, Bath, 1740), lxviii. Eighteenth-century
English writers were notoriously inconsistent in their
use of punctuation and capitalization. Throughout
this book, in order to make some of the language
more intelligible and easier to read, I have sometimes
modified it by using the appropriate punctuation and
capitalization.

5. He added, "But what epicure will ever regard it? For
the man 'talks against good eating and drinking'!"
Journal entry, February 12, 1742, Jackson, *The Works
of John Wesley*, 1:363.

6. See Kenneth J. Collins, *A Real Christian: The Life of
John Wesley* (Nashville: Abingdon, 1999), 30; and
Malony, "John Wesley's Primitive Physick," 150–51.

See also, "A Second Letter to the Reverend Dr. Fee,"
Jackson, *The Works of John Wesley*, 8:506 ("It was from
an ancient sect of Physicians, who we were supposed
to resemble in our regular diet and exercise, that we
were originally styled 'Methodists' ").

7. See Randy Maddox, "Reclaiming the Eccentric Parent,"
in *Inward and Outward Health: John Wesley's Holistic
Concept of Medical Science, the Environment and Holy
Living*, ed. Deborah Madden (London: Epworth, 2008),
16–17; and Randy Maddox, "Celebrating the Whole
Wesley: A Legacy for Contemporary Wesleyans,"
Methodist History 43, no. 2 (2005), 85: "Wesley longed
for Christians to see that participation in God's present
work of holistic salvation includes nurturing not only
our souls, but our bodies, and addressing both of these
dimensions in our outreach to others."

8. "A Plain Account of the People Called Methodists,"
(1748), Jackson, *The Works of John Wesley*, 8:264.

9. Randy Maddox, "John Wesley on Holistic Health
and Healing" *Methodist History* 46, no. 1 (2007): 18.
A Primitive Physic is also frequently cited herein.
Although early editions of the book were titled
A Primitive Physick, for consistency, I use only the
spelling "Physic," unless the context requires the use of
the other spelling.

10. Maddox, "Reclaiming the Eccentric Parent," in *Inward
and Outward Health*, 19. By comparison, William
Buchan's *Domestic Medicine* (1769) sold for six
shillings. Deborah Madden, "Wesley as Advisor on
Health and Healing" in *Cambridge Companion to John
Wesley*, ed. Maddox and Vickers, 182.

11. Letter to Mr. Merryweather, January 24, 1760, *The
Works of John Wesley*, ed. Jackson, 12:269.

12. David Stewart, "John Wesley, The Physician," *Wesleyan
Theological Journal* 4, no.1 (1969): 35–36; Madden,
"Wesley as Advisor on Health and Healing," 184. See
also Deborah Madden, *A Cheap and Safe Natural*

*Medicine: Religion, Medicine and Culture in John
Wesley's Primitive Physick* (New York: Rodopi, 2007).

Chapter 3

1. Michael Pollan, *In Defense of Food: An Eater's Manifesto*
   (London: Penguin, 2008), 1.
2. Michael Pollan, *Food Rules: An Eater's Manual*
   (London: Penguin, 2009), xii–iv.
3. "Upon Our Lord's Sermon on the Mount, Discourse
   VII," *The Works of John Wesley*, ed. Jackson, 5:359.
4. H. Newton Malony, "John Wesley's Primitive Physick,"
   Journal of Health Psychology 1, no.2 (1996), 150.
5. "A Word to an Unhappy Woman," *The Works of John
   Wesley*, ed. Jackson, 11:172.
6. "The General Spread of the Gospel," *The Works of
   John Wesley*, ed. Jackson, 6:288. For an extended
   examination of Wesley's eschatological views in his
   later years, see Randy Maddox, "Nurturing the New
   Creation: Reflections on a Wesleyan Trajectory,"
   in *Wesleyan Perspectives on the New Creation*, ed.
   M. Douglas Meeks (Nashville: Kingswood, 2004).
7. Margaret Flowers, "A Wesleyan Theology of
   Environmental Stewardship" in *Inward and Outward*,
   ed. Madden, 73.
8. "God has . . . entrusted us with our bodies (those
   exquisitely wrought machines, so 'fearfully and
   wonderfully made') with all the powers and members
   thereof. He has entrusted us with the organs of sense;
   of sight, hearing, and the rest: But none of these are
   given us as our own, to be employed according to our
   own will. None of these are lent us in such a sense
   as to leave us at liberty to use them as we please for
   a season. No: We have received them on these very
   terms,—that, as long as they abide with us, we should
   employ them all in that very manner, and no other,
   which he appoints." "The Good Steward," *The Works of
   John Wesley*, ed. Jackson, 6:138.

9. "On Worldly Folly," *The Works of John Wesley*, ed. Jackson, 7:307.

10. Malony, "John Wesley's Primitive Physick," 151.

11. George Cheyne, *An Essay of Health and Long Life* (London: printed for George Strahan; and J. Leake, Bath, 1724), 4, available on the website of Eighteenth Century Collections Online, http://quod.lib.umich .edu/e/ecco/004834818.0001.000?rgn=main ;view=fulltext.

12. John Wesley, *Explanatory Notes upon the Old Testament*, Exodus 20:13. Viewed at *John Wesley's Notes on the Bible*, Wesley Center Online, Northwest Nazarene University, http://wesley.nnu.edu/john -wesley/john-wesleys-notes-on-the-bible/notes-on-the -second-book-of-moses-called-exodus/#Chapter+XX (accessed February 18, 2014).

13. Ibid.; Deuteronomy 5:17, http://wesley.nnu.edu /john-wesley/john-wesleys-notes-on-the-bible/notes -on-the-fifth-book-of-moses-called-deuteronomy /#Chapter%2BV (accessed February 18, 2014). Note that Wesley loathed suicide, referring to it as "self-murder," and as a "horrid" and "execrable" crime. Demonstrating how strongly he felt, in his 1790 treatise "On Suicide" Wesley cited the Spartan precedent of exposing the naked bodies of suicide victims in the streets, and went so far as to urge that "a law be made and vigorously executed, that the body of every self-murderer, lord or peasant, be hanged in chains." For Wesley to equate the knowing consumption of unhealthy food to suicide was therefore no small matter.

14. Cheyne, *An Essay of Health*, 4–5.

15. Rebekah Miles, "Happiness, Holiness, and the Moral Life in John Wesley," in *Cambridge Companion to John Wesley*, ed. Maddox and Vickers, 221.

16. "Calvinist Methodists and other Calvinists, for example, objected to Wesley's approach, contending that preachers should stick to saving souls alone." Maddox, "Reclaiming the Eccentric Parent," in *Inward and Outward Health*, ed. Madden, 17. See also Madden, *A Cheap and Safe Natural Medicine*, 80 ("Wesley was criticized by the Calvinists for the time he spent engaged in medical activity—time better spent, they argued, studying Scripture").

Chapter 4

1. Quoted in Howard Snyder, *The Radical Wesley: The Patterns and Practices of a Movement Maker* (Franklin, TN: Seedbed Publishing, 2014), 60.

2. "Overweight" is defined as having a body mass index (BMI) of 25 or higher; "obesity" is defined as a BMI of 30 or higher. Centers for Disease Control and Prevention, "Defining Overweight and Obesity," April, 27, 2012, http://www.cdc.gov/obesity/adult /defining.html. As of 2010, an estimated 68.8 percent of Americans were overweight or obese. Katherine M. Flegal, et al., "Prevalence of Obesity and Trends in the Distribution of Body Mass Index among US Adults, 1999–2010," *Journal of the American Medical Association* 307, no. 5 (2012): 491–97.

3. Ryan K. Masters, et al., "The Impact of Obesity on US Mortality Levels: The Importance of Age and Cohort Factors in Population Estimates," *American Journal of Public Health* 103, no. 10 (October 2013): 1895–901.

4. Research has shown that as weight increases to reach the levels referred to as "overweight" and "obesity," the risks for the following conditions also increase: coronary heart disease, type 2 diabetes, cancers (endometrial, breast, and colon), hypertension (high blood pressure), dyslipidemia (for example, high

total cholesterol or high levels of triglycerides), stroke, liver, and gallbladder disease, sleep apnea and respiratory problems, osteoarthritis (a degeneration of cartilage and its underlying bone within a joint), and gynecological problems (abnormal menses, infertility). Centers for Disease Control and Prevention, "Causes and Consequences," upd. April 27, 2012, http://www .cdc.gov/obesity/adult/causes/index.html.

5. "An Estimate of the Manners of the Present Times," 7 (1782), *The Works of John Wesley*, ed. Jackson, 11:158.

6. "Upon the Lord's Sermon on the Mount Discourse VII," III 5, *The Works of John Wesley*, ed. Jackson, 5:349–50.

7. "Queries Respecting the Methodists," *The Works of John Wesley*, ed. Jackson, 13:510.

8. "The Rich Man and Lazarus," *The Works of John Wesley*, ed. Jackson 7:250.

9. H. Newton Malony, "John Wesley's Primitive Physick," *Journal of Health Psychology* 1, no. 2 (1996): 151. To avoid nervous disorders Wesley advised that his preachers "take as little meat, drink and sleep as nature will bear." "Minutes of Several Conversations between the Rev. Mr. Wesley and Others; From the Year 1744 to the Year 1789," *The Works of John Wesley*, ed. Jackson, 8:314.

10. David Grumett, *Theology on the Menu: Asceticism, Meat and Christian Diet* (New York: Routledge, 2010), 61, 63. See also Philip W. Ott, "John Wesley on Health as Wholeness," *Journal of Religion and Health*, no. 1 (1991): 200–201.

11. Deborah Madden, *A Cheap and Safe Natural Medicine: Religion, Medicine and Culture in John Wesley's Primitive Physick* (New York: Rodopi, 2007), 41.

12. See, for example, "Letter to James McDonald" dated October 23, 1790, *The Works of John Wesley*, ed. Jackson, 13:120.

13. "Minutes of Several Conversations between the Rev. Mr. Wesley and Others; From the Year 1744 to the Year 1789," *The Works of John Wesley*, ed. Jackson, 8:324.

14. Wesley, "A Plain Account of Christian Perfection," *The Works of John Wesley*, ed. Jackson, 11:422. Note that for Wesley intemperance can be reflected both in the quantity and the quality of the food one eats. Eating unhealthy food, even in moderation, would still reflect an absence of temperance.

15. "Upon the Lord's Sermon on the Mount Discourse VII." *The Works of John Wesley*, ed. Jackson, 5:356.

16. "On Dress," *The Works of John Wesley*, ed. Jackson, 7:20. Even though hunger and food insecurity continue to exist, in the developed world they are not the major problems they were in Wesley's day (indeed the developed world has the first population in history where the poor are often obese, suffering not from too little food, but rather too little *nutritious* food); in many parts of the world people continue to suffer from hunger and starvation, while our society grows ever fatter. Today there are more people in the world who are overweight than there are who are hungry. Daniel Imhoff, *The CAFO Reader: The Tragedy of Industrial Animal Factories*, ed. Daniel Imhoff (Berkeley: University of California Press, 2010), 81, citing Raj Patel, *Stuffed and Starved: The Hidden Battle for the World's Food System* (Brooklyn: Melville House, 2008), 1.

17. "Upon the Lord's Sermon on the Mount Discourse IV," *The Works of John Wesley*, ed. Jackson, 5:309.

18. See Bill McKibben, *Deep Economy: The Wealth of Communities and the Durable Future* (New York: Times Books, 2007), for an extended argument and analysis.

19. Ellen Gustafson, *We the Eaters: If We Change Dinner We Can Change the World* (New York: Rodale, 2014).

20. "Garrison Keillor on Those People Called Methodists,"
    February 13, 2007, cited on the Ben Witherington
    blog, http://benwitherington.blogspot.com/2007/02
    /garrison-keillor-on-those-people-called.html. Or
    like the Facebook post by the UMC Foundation on
    February 24, 2014 showing a plate of fried chicken
    with the caption "United Methodists—when 2 or
    more are gathered together—a chicken dies. Is that
    why it crossed the road? It was in front of a Methodist
    church?"

21. R. J. Proeschold-Bell and S. H. LeGrand, "High Rates
    of Obesity and Chronic Disease among United
    Methodist Clergy," *Obesity* 18 (2010): 1867–70, in
    Kate Rugani, "Body and Soul" *Faith & Leadership*,
    July 8, 2010, http://www.faithandleadership.com
    /features/articles/body-and-soul.

22. Ben Witherington III, *The Rest of Life: Rest, Studying,
    Eating, Play and Sex from a Kingdom Perspective* (Grand
    Rapids: Eerdmans, 2013), 65–66. One study has found
    that among American Christians, Baptists are the most
    likely to be obese. Ken Ferraro, "Study Finds Faithful
    Less Likely to Pass the Plate," August 24, 2006, Purdue
    University News, https://news.uns.purdue.edu/htm
    l4ever/2006/060824.Ferraro.obesity.html.

23. Centers for Disease Control and Prevention, "Adult
    Obesity Facts," http://www.cdc.gov/obesity/data
    /adult.html.

24. James Harnish, *Simple Rules for Money: John Wesley
    on Earning, Saving and Giving* (Nashville: Abingdon,
    2009), 41–42. See Ferraro, "Study Finds Faithful Less
    Likely to Pass the Plate."

25. Marla Paul, "Religious Young Adults Become Obese
    By Middle Age," Northwestern University website,
    March 23, 2011, http://www.northwestern.edu
    /newscenter/stories/2011/03/religious-young-adults
    -obese.html.

26. *A Primitive Physic*, preface, II 4, *The Works of John Wesley*, ed. Jackson, 14:314.

27. Cheyne, *An Essay of Good Health*, 34. Wesley seems to have misunderstood Cheyne's advice, however, as this is the quantity of food that Cheyne recommended for those *not* engaged in studious or intellectual pursuits. Cheyne wrote, "Those engaged in sedentary professions or intellectual studies must lessen this quantity if they would preserve their health and the freedom of their spirits long. Studious and sedentary men must of necessity eat and drink a great deal less than those very same men might do were they engaged in an active life." Ibid. Cheyne's advice to sedentary men was: "I advise therefore all gentlemen of a sedentary life and of learned professions to use such abstinence as possibly they can consistent with the preservation of their strength and freedom of spirits . . . either by lessening one half of their usual quantity of animal food and strong liquors . . . or by living a due time wholly upon vegetable diet, such as sago, rice, pudding and the like and drinking only a little wine and water." Ibid. In any event, Wesley (and Cheyne) recognized that those with sedentary lifestyles should eat less than those with active lifestyles, advice that is as valid today as ever.

28. Cheyne devoted an entire chapter of his book *The English Malady* to a discussion of exercise as a means of preventing illness and disease. George Cheyne, *The English malady: or a Treatise of nervous diseases of all kinds; as spleen, vapours, lowness of spirits, hypochondriacal, and hysterical distempers, etc*, (London: G. Strahan; Bath: J. Leake, 1734), 172ff.

29. Henry D. Rack, *Reasonable Enthusiast: John Wesley and the Rise of Methodism* (London: Epworth, 2002), 183. "In the year 1769 I weighed an hundred and twenty two pounds. In 1783 I weighed not a pound more or

less. I doubt whether such another instance is to be found in Great Britain." Journal Entry, November 17, 1783, *The Works of John Wesley*, ed. Jackson, 4:264.

30. Charles Wallace, "Simple and Recollected: John Wesley's Life-Style," *Religion in Life* 46.2 (1977): 200.

31. Journal, June 28, 1788, *The Works of John Wesley*, ed. Jackson, 4:427.

32. A. Skevington Wood, *The Burning Heart, John Wesley: Evangelist* (Lexington: Emeth, 2007), 135, quoting journal entry of that date.

33. "An Estimate of the Manners of the Present Times" (1782), *The Works of John Wesley*, ed. Jackson, 11:156; "Thoughts on Nervous Disorders, Particularly That Which Is Usually Termed Lowness of Spirits," *The Works of John Wesley*, ed. Jackson, 11:520.

34. *Primitive Physic*, Preface, *The Works of John Wesley*, ed. Jackson, 14:308. See also W. Phillip Ott, "A Corner of History: John Wesley and the Non-Naturals." *Preventive Medicine* 9 (n.d.): 578.

35. Ibid., 14:315.

36. *The Works of John Wesley*, ed. Jackson, 12:343.

37. Viewed at http://wesley.nnu.edu/john-wesley/the -letters-of-john-wesley/wesleys-letters-1780a/ (accessed February 10, 2014).

38. Preface to Wesley's *Extract from Dr. Cadogan's Dissertation on the Gout and all Chronic Diseases*, 10. *The Works of John Wesley*, ed. Jackson, 14:268.

39. "The Character of a Methodist," 15, *The Works of John Wesley*, ed. Jackson, 8:345

Chapter 5

1. Hilda Kean, *Animal Rights: Political and Social Change in Britain since 1800* (London: Rektion, 1998), 24.

2. Tony Collins, John Martin, and Wray Vamplew, eds., *Encyclopedia of Traditional British Rural Sports* (London; New York: Routledge, 2005), 52.

3. Carrie Hirbar, *Understanding Concentrated Animal Feeding Operations and Their Impact on Communities* (Bowling Green, OH: National Association of Local Boards of Health, 2010), 1.

4. Daniel Imhoff, introduction to *The CAFO Reader: The Tragedy of Industrial Animal Factories*, ed. Daniel Imhoff (Berkeley: University of California Press, 2010), xiv.

5. Ibid.

6. Sandra Richter, "And What Does God Require?" *Blessed Earth* (blog), http://www.blessedearth.org /category/blogs/sandy-richter/ (accessed February 8, 2014).

7. Elise Titia Gieling, Rebecca Elizabeth Nordquist, and Franz Josef van der Staay, "Assessing Learning and Memory in Pigs," *Animal Cognition*, 14, no. 2 (March 2011): 151–73, http://www.ncbi.nlm.nih.gov/pmc /articles/PMC3040303/.

8. See Bernard E. Rollin, "Farm Factories: The End of Animal Husbandry," in *The CAFO Reader*, ed. Imhoff, 23.

9. Fabian Tepper, "The New Ethics of Eating," *Christian Science Monitor*, December 7, 2014, http://www .csmonitor.com/USA/Society/2014/1207/The -new-ethics-of-eating.

10. Ibid.

11. "Upon the Lord's Sermon on the Mount: Discourse III," *The Works of John Wesley*, ed. Jackson, 5:283.

12. "Minutes of Several Conversations between the Rev. Mr. Wesley and Others; From the Year 1744 to the Year 1789," *The Works of John Wesley*, ed. Jackson, 8:318.

13. Susan Hogan, "Methodism Founder Inspires Christian Vegetarians," January 21, 2010 (quoting Randy Maddox), http://www.umc.org/site/apps /nlnet/content3.aspx?c=lwL4KnN1LtH&b=525966 9&ct=7867623; no longer accessible.

14. Kean, *Animal Rights*, 54.

15. "On the Education of Children," *The Works of John Wesley*, ed. Jackson, 7:98.

16. Quoted in Peter Harrison, "Descartes on Animals." *Philosophical Quarterly* 42, no. 167 (1992): 219.

17. Wesley, *A Survey of the Wisdom of God in the Creation: A Compendium of Natural Philosophy in Two Volumes*, pt. 2, chap. 6 (1763), Wesley Center Online, http://wesley.nnu.edu/john-wesley/a-compendium-of-natural-philosophy/chapter-6-general-observations-and-reflections (accessed February 8, 2014).

18. Flowers, Margaret G., *Inward and Outward Health John Wesley's Holistic Concept of Medical Science, the Environment and Holy Living*, ed. Deborah Madden (London: Epworth, 2008), 76.

19. "The General Deliverance" *The Works of John Wesley*, ed. Jackson, 6:251. Note, however that although Wesley is often quoted as having written, "I believe in my heart that faith in Jesus Christ can and will lead us beyond an exclusive concern for the well-being of other human beings to the broader concern for the well-being of the birds in our backyards, the fish in our rivers, and every living creature on the face of the earth," the quote does not appear to be legitimate. The quote appears on hundreds of websites and in numerous books. None of these texts cite any Wesley source document, however, nor did I discover any such quote in my own research. The language does not seem characteristic of Wesley, and it seems unlikely that he would reference "backyards." It is a pity this bogus quote is so well circulated, considering there is no shortage of legitimate quotes from Wesley expressing the same sentiment.

20. "The Approbation of God's Works," *The Works of John Wesley*, ed. Jackson, 6:212.

21. See Randy L. Maddox, "John Wesley's Precedent for Theological Engagement with the Natural Sciences," *Wesleyan Theological Journal* 44, no.1 (2009): 48. Maddox noted that Wesley shared the sentiment of his friend and mentor George Cheyne, who had in 1740 written in his *An Essay on Regimen*: "It is utterly incredible that any creature . . . should come into this state of being and suffering for no other purpose than we see them attain here. . . . There must be some infinitely beautiful, wise, and good scene remaining for all sentient and intelligent beings, the discovery of which will ravish and astonish us one day." But, Maddox added, "Wesley's proposal about this scene would likely have astonished even Cheyne!"

22. Maddox, "Nurturing the New Creation," in *Wesleyan Perspectives on the New Creation*, ed. Meeks, 47.

23. Ibid., 49.

24. John Lenton, *John Wesley's Preachers: A Social and Statistical Analysis of the British and Irish Preachers Who Entered the Methodist Itinerary Before 1791* (Eugene, OR: Wipf and Stock, 2009), 122.

25. David Grumett, "A Christian Diet," *Christian Century* 127, no. 7 (2010): 61; Wallace, "Simple and Recollected," 200–201.

26. Wesley was influenced by Cheyne, who in his *Essay on Regimen* recommended eating "temperate" amounts of animal food until age fifty, after which "animal food suppers" should be given up. After age sixty Cheyne advised that a person should eat no "animal food." Cheyne, *Essay on Regimen*, xxx.

27. *A Primitive Physic*, 3, *The Works of John Wesley*, ed. Jackson, 14:309. Here too Wesley specifically notes that God does not require a strictly vegetarian diet.

28. There is, however, evidence that pigs fed genetically modified grains are less healthy than those that are

not. Carey Gillam, "Scientists Say New Study Shows Pig Health Hurt by GMO Feed," June 11, 2013, http://www.reuters.com/article/2013/06/11/us-gmo -pigs-study-idUSBRE95A14K20130611. Nearly all of the animal feed produced today is made with genetically modified grains.

29. Michael Pollan, "Power Steer: On the Trail of Industrial Beef," in *The CAFO Reader*, ed. Imhoff, 99.

30. See, for example, H. D. Karsten, et al. "Vitamins A, E, and Fatty Acid Composition of the Eggs of Caged Hens and Pastured Hens," *Renewable Agriculture and Food Systems* 25 (March 2010): 45–54.

31. See, for example, Cynthia A. Daley, et al. "A Review of Fatty Acid Profiles and Antioxidant Content in Grass-Fed and Grain-Fed Beef," *Nutrition Journal* 9, no. 10 (2010). For a summary of some of the nutritional advantages of grass-fed beef, see Tanya Denckla Cobb, *Reclaiming Our Food: How the Grassroots Food Movement Is Changing the Way We Eat* (East Adams, MA: Storey, 2011), 237. Regarding the distinctive taste of grass-fed beef, see Pollan, "Power Steer," 107.

32. Cheyne, *The English Malady*, 50.

33. Cheyne, *An Essay of Health and Long Life*, 24, 28, 73.

34. George Burnap Fiske, *Poultry Feeding and Fattening* (New York: O. Judd, 1904), 92. This type of force-feeding is still used to produce foie gras, for example.

35. Cheyne, *An Essay on Health and Long Life*, 28.

36. Wendell Berry, *What Are People For?* (New York: North Point, 1990), 151.

37. H. Newton Malony, "John Wesley's Primitive Physick," *Journal of Health Psychology* 1, no. 2 (1996): 150 (emphasis added).

Chapter 6

1. Michelle Brandt, "Little Evidence of Health Benefits from Organic Food, Stanford Study Shows," Stanford

Medicine News Center, September 3, 2012, http://
med.stanford.edu/ism/2012/september/organic.html;
Kenneth Chang, "Parsing of Data Led to Mixed
Messages on Organic Food's Value," *New York
Times*, October 15, 2012, http://www.nytimes
.com/2012/10/16/science/stanford-organic-food
-study-and-vagaries-of-meta-analyses.html?_r=0
(accessed February 8, 2014); Damian Carrington and
George Arnett, "Clear Differences between Organic
and Non-organic Food, Study Finds," *Guardian*
(UK), July 11, 2014, http://www.theguardian
.com/environment/2014/jul/11/organic-food
-more-antioxidants-study?CMP=twt_gu.

2. Mayo Clinic Staff, "Organic Foods: Are They Safer?
   More Nutritious?" Mayo Clinic website, September 7,
   2012, http://www.mayoclinic.org/organic-food
   /ART-20043880?pg=1.

3. Randy Maddox, "John Wesley on Holistic Health and
   Healing," *Methodist History* 46, no. 1 (2007): 24.

4. Joe Gorman, "John Wesley and Depression in an Age
   of Melancholy," *Wesleyan Theological Journal* 34, no. 2
   (1999): 74.

5. Gordon Gadsby and Francis Dewhurst, "John Wesley's
   Contribution to the Evolution of Alternative and
   Holistic Healing," *Epworth Review* 26, no. 1 (1999):
   96–98.

6. Preface to *The Desideratum: Or, Electricity Made Plain
   and Useful*, 4, *The Works of John Wesley*, ed. Jackson,
   1: 242.

7. Melanie Dobson Hughes, "The Holistic Way: John
   Wesley's Practical Piety as a Resource for Integrated
   Healthcare," *Journal of Religion & Health* 47, no. 2
   (2008): 243.

8. Maddox, "John Wesley on Holistic Health and
   Healing," 24.

9. Ellen Davis, *Scripture, Culture and Agriculture: An Agrarian Reading of the Bible* (New York: Cambridge University Press, 2009), 87.

10. Vandana Shiva, "Move over, God, the Biotech Companies are Here," *CounterCurrents.org*, May 29, 2013, http://www.countercurrents.org/shiva 290513.htm.

11. Preface, *A Primitive Physic*.

12. Foodfacts.com, http://www.foodfacts.com/ci /nutritionfacts/brownie-and-cake-products/little -debbie-oatmeal-cream-pies-12-pack-16-oz/142267 (accessed April 13, 2015).

13. See Kristy Storrar, "59 Ingredients in Strawberry Milkshake but No Strawberries," *Mirror* (UK), April 25, 2006, http://www.mirror.co.uk/news/uk -news/59-ingredients-in-strawberry-milkshake---622350. The ingredient list reads like some sort of chemical stew: "Amyl acetate, amyl butyrate, amyl valerate, anethol, anisyl formate, benzyl acetate, benzyl isobutyrate, butyric acid, cinnamyl isobutyrate, cinnamyl valerate, cognac essential oil, diacetyl, dipropyl ketone, ethyl butyrate, ethyl cinnamate, ethyl heptanoate, ethyl heptylate, ethyl lactate, ethyl methylphenylglycidate, ethyl nitrate, ethylpropionate, ethyl valerate, heliotropin, hydroxyphrenyl-2-butanone (10% solution in alcohol), ionone, isobutyl anthranilate, isobutyl butyrate, lemon essential oil, maltol, 4-methylace-tophenone, methyl anthranilate, methyl benzoate, methyl cinnamate, methyl heptine carbonate, methyl naphtyl ketone, methyl salicylate, mint essential oil, neroli essential oil, nerolin, neryl isobutyrate, orris butter, phenethyl alcohol, undecalactone, rum ether, rose, vanillin and solvent."

14. Pollan, *Food Rules*, chaps. 3, 6, 7.

15. Theodore Runyon, *The New Creation: John Wesley's Theology Today* (Nashville: Abingdon, 1998), 200.

16. Kenneth Milton Loyer, "'And to Crown All': John Wesley on Union with God in the New Creation," *Methodist Review* 1 (2009): 119.

17. Howard Snyder, *Yes in Christ: Wesleyan Reflections on Gospel, Mission and Culture,* (Toronto: Clements Academic, 2010), 91–92.

18. Ibid., 95–96.

19. Randy Maddox, *Responsible Grace: John Wesley's Practical Theology* (Nashville: Kingswood, 1994), 246–47.

20. Maddox, "Wesley's Engagement with the Natural Sciences," in *Cambridge Companion*, ed. Maddox and Vickers, 174

21. John Wesley, "The Good Steward," *The Works of John Wesely*, ed. Jackson, 6:137.

22. Runyon, *The New Creation*, 207.

23. Leo Horrigan, Jay Graham, and Shawn McKenzie, "Antibiotic Drug Abuse: CAFOs Are Squandering Vital Human Medicines" in *The CAFO Reader*, ed. Imhoff, 256–57.

24. Ibid., 258.

25. "What's in That Pork? We Found Antibiotic-Resistant Bacteria and Traces of a Veterinary Drug," *Consumer Reports*, January 2013, http://www.consumerreports.org/cro/pork0113.htm.

26. David Schardt, "Antibiotic Resistance: Wasting a Precious Life Saver," *Nutrition Action Newsletter*, May 1, 2013, http://www.thefreelibrary.com/Antibiotic+resistance%3A+wasting+a+precious+life+saver.-a0329364714.

Chapter 7

1. Roberto A. Ferdman, "A map of all the countries that contribute to a single jar of Nutella," Quartz, December 11, 2013, http://qz.com/156163/a-map-of-all-the-countries-that-contribute-to-a-single-jar-of-nutella/.

2. "Just 73 Ingredients," Discoverfood.org, March 7, 2012, http://www.discoverfood.org/2012/03/whats -in-a-mcdonalds-big-mac-just-73-ingredients.html; no longer accessible.

3. See Melanie Warner, *Pandora's Lunchbox: How Processed Foods Took Over the American Meal* (New York: Scribner, 2013), 81–82.

4. Howard Snyder and Joel Scandrette, *Salvation Means Creation Healed: The Ecology of Sin and Grace: Overcoming the Divorce Between Heaven and Earth* (Eugene, OR: Wipf and Stock, Cascade, 2011), 153.

5. George Cheyne, *The English malady: or a Treatise of nervous diseases of all kinds; as spleen, vapours, lowness of spirits, hypochondriacal, and hysterical distempers, etc,* (London: G. Strahan; Bath: J. Leake, 1734), 156, 216.

6. Ibid., 156–57.

7. Stephen Martinez, et al., "Local Food Systems: Concepts, Impacts and Issues," *Economic Research Report* 87 (May 2010), http://www.ers.usda.gov /publications/err-economic-research-report/err97 .aspx#.VBeGJpRdUdU.

8. "National Sins and Miseries," II 3, *The Works of John Wesley*, ed. Jackson, 7:406.

9. "Thoughts on the Present Scarcity of Provisions." John Wesley Sermon.

10. Charles Wallace and Jeremy Gregory, "Eating and Drinking with John Wesley: The Logic of His Practice." *Bulletin of the John Rylands University Library of Manchester* 85, nos. 2, 3 (2003): 148.

11. "The Use of Money," *The Works of John Wesley*, ed. Jackson, 6:128.

Chapter 8

1. "An Address to the Clergy," *The Works of John Wesley*, ed. Jackson, 10:498.

2. Tanya Denckla Cobb, *Reclaiming Our Food: How the Grassroots Food Movement Is Changing the Way We Eat* (East Adams, MA: Storey, 2011), 8–9.
3. "National Sins and Miseries," *The Works of John Wesley*, ed. Jackson, 7:406.
4. Geoff Andrews, *Slow Food Story: Politics and Pleasure* (London: Pluto Press, 2008), 17–20.
5. Ibid., 68.
6. Wesley, "On God's Vineyard," *The Works of John Wesley*, ed. Jackson, 7:212.
7. Charles Wallace and Jeremy Gregory, "Eating and Drinking with John Wesley: The Logic of His Practice," *Bulletin of the John Rylands University Library of Manchester* 85, nos. 2, 3 (2003): 146.
8. "A Plain Account of Christian Perfection," *The Works of John Wesley*, ed. Jackson, 11:399. Note also that Wesley's comparison of pleasing to unpleasing food presumes that both are "equally wholesome." Thus while he would obviously have no objection to a Christian choosing fresh, locally grown food over its alternative, he would in all events object to the eating of any food that is not "wholesome."
9. "Thoughts on a Single Life," *The Works of John Wesley*, ed. Jackson, 11:461.
10. Andrews, *Slow Food Story*, 39.
11. Samuel J. Rogal, *Essays on John Wesley and His Contemporaries: The Texture of 18th Century English Culture* (Lewiston, NY: Edwin Mellen, 2007), 227.
12. Stephen Tomkins, *John Wesley: A Biography* (Minneapolis: Eerdmans, 2003), 199.
13. "An Earnest Appeal to Men of Reason and Religion," *The Works of John Wesley*, ed. Jackson, 8:40.
14. "Advice to the People Called Methodists with Regard to Dress," *The Works of John Wesley*, ed. Jackson, 11:477.

15. "The Use of Money," *The Works of John Wesley*, ed. Jackson, 6:133–34.

16. "Upon Our Lord's Sermon on the Mount, Discourse VIII," *The Works of John Wesley*, ed. Jackson, 5:367.

17. "Upon Our Lord's Sermon on the Mount, Discourse VII," *The Works of John Wesley*, ed. Jackson, 5:359.

18. Ronald H. Stone, *John Wesley's Life and Ethics* (Nashville: Abingdon, 2001), 223.

19. USDA Economic Research Service, "Food Expenditures," http://www.ers.usda.gov/data-products/food-expenditures.aspx#.UtXX3NJDsdU (accessed February 8, 2014). Note that for food eaten at home the amount was a mere 5.7 percent.

20. Shannon Jung, *Food for Life: The Spirituality and Ethics of Eating* (Minneapolis: Fortress, 2004), 81.

21. Mayuree Rayo, et al. "Do healthier foods and diet patterns cost more than less healthy options? A systematic review and meta-analysis" *BMJ Open* 3 (December 2013): e004277, http://bmjopen.bmj.com/content/3/12/e004277.full.

22. Jennifer R. Ayres, *Good Food: Grounded Practical Theology* (Waco: Baylor University Press, 2013), 101.

23. Norman Wirzba, "Eating in Ignorance," *Christian Century* 129, no. 11 (May 30, 2012): 24.

24. Michael Moss, "The Extraordinary Science of Addictive Junk Food," *New York Times Magazine*, February 20, 2013, 1.

25. Ibid., 240.

26. Melanie Warner, *Pandora's Lunchbox: How Processed Foods Took Over the American Meal* (New York: Scribner, 2013), 219.

Chapter 9

1. Randy Maddox, "John Wesley Says, 'Take Care of Yourself,'" *Faith & Leadership*, July 31, 2012, http://

www.faithandleadership.com/randy-maddox-john
-wesley-says-take-care-yourself.

2. Matthew Sleeth, *Serve God, Save the Planet: A Christian Call to Action* (White River Junction, VT: Chelsea Green, 2006), 115.

3. "A Plain Account of Christian Perfection," *The Works of John Wesley*, ed. Jackson, 11:438.

4. "Upon the Lord's Sermon on the Mount, Discourse IV," John Wesley, *Thirteen Discourses on the Sermon on the Mount* (Franklin, TN: Seedbed, 2014), 82.

5. "The Character of a Methodist," *The Works of John Wesley*, ed. Jackson, 8:345.

6. Visit http://beeckencenter.sewanee.edu/programs /faith-farm-food-network

7. "Following Christ as a Lunatic Grass Farmer: An Interview with Joel Salatin," RedLetterChristians.org, July 7, 2014, http://www.redletterchristians.org /following-christ-lunatic-grass-farmer-interview-joel -salatin/.

8. C. Christopher Smith and John Pattison, *Slow Church: Cultivating Community in the Patient Way of Jesus* (Downers Grove, IL: InterVarsity Press, 2014).

9. John Joseph Thompson, *Jesus, Bread and Chocolate: Crafting a Hand-Made Faith in a Mass-Market World* (Grand Rapids: Zondervan, 2015).

10. James Harnish, *Simple Rules for Money: John Wesley on Earning, Saving and Giving* (Nashville: Abingdon, 2009), 41–42.

11. Ben Witherington III, *The Rest of Life: Rest, Studying, Eating, Play and Sex from a Kingdom Perspective* (Grand Rapids: Eerdmans, 2013), 65ff.

12. Ibid., 66.

13. Howard Snyder and Joel Scandrette, *Salvation Means Creation Healed: The Ecology of Sin and Grace: Overcoming the Divorce Between Heaven and Earth* (Eugene, OR: Wipf and Stock, Cascade, 2011), 153.

14. Ibid., 202, 223.
15. Ibid., 202.
16. Ayres, 64–65.
17. The United Methodist Church, The Social Principles of the United Methodist Church, ¶ 160G; ¶163H ("The concentration of the food supply for the many into the hands of the few raises global questions of justice that cry out for vigilance and action."); ¶162. III; "The United Methodist Church, Justice, and World Hunger (#4051, 2008 BOR)," http://umc-gbcs.org /resolutions/the-united-methodist-church-justice-and -world-hunger-4051-2008-bor; "Health and Wholeness (#3202, 2008 BOR)," http://umc-gbcs.org/resolutions /health-and-wholeness-3202-2008-bor (accessed February 10, 2014).
18. Maddox, "John Wesley Says, 'Take Care of Yourself.' "
19. "The General Spread of the Gospel," *The Works of John Wesley*, ed. Jackson, 6:288.
20. John Wesley, "Letter to a Friend Concerning Tea," *The Works of John Wesley*, ed. Jackson, 11:513.